MANUAL
OF SEX EDUCATION

FOR PARENTS, TEACHERS AND STUDENTS

By
C. F. DERSTINE
BISHOP, EVANGELIST, AUTHOR, EDITOR
of *Comments on World News*
in *Christian Monitor*

SECOND EDITION

ZONDERVAN PUBLISHING HOUSE
GRAND RAPIDS MICHIGAN

PRINTED IN THE UNITED STATES OF AMERICA BY THE
ZONDERVAN PUBLISHING HOUSE
EIGHT FORTY-SEVEN OTTAWA AVENUE
GRAND RAPIDS, MICHIGAN

FOREWORD

THIS BOOK does not aim at a systematic technical
treatment of the physiological phases of sexual life—this
part has been left to specialists. It is a "Manual"—
that is, a compact treatment of this important subject—
for the average parent and teacher of children and
youth, in which he may find practical assistance in the
instruction of youth about the facts of reproduction.
Simply, it tells how to tell the story of life; how to
answer the most beautiful question: "Where did we
come from, Mother dear?"

Horace Mann said of himself: "I was taught all about
the motions of the planets as carefully as if they would
have been in danger of getting off the track if I had
not known about their orbits, but about my own origina-
tion I was left in profound ignorance."

The superintendent of a Rescue Home in one of our
cities made it a point to discover the primary cause
for the downfall of each girl. This was her finding:
Not one of the two hundred had received any instructions from their mother or anyone else about their
sexual impulses. The most that any received was the
threadbare injunction to be a "good girl."

Fathers, mothers and teachers not prepared to teach

this vital and fundamental subject should avail themselves of suitable books. Most parents find it difficult to present the facts and answer the questions asked. Chapters II and III are arranged to read to children from five to twelve years of age. The whole book has been written with the intent of making it a proper one to hand to the youth and maiden at a later period of life.

Teachers of sex must be on guard against two extreme attitudes. First, "too much and too early"; second, "too little and too late." The first mistake is unwise; the second may be fatal.

The author has been a student, teacher and lecturer on sex education themes for some thirty years. In these lectures he has addressed audiences from the Atlantic to the Pacific coasts; in churches, high schools and colleges. Everywhere there has been an insistent demand for sex books—sane, sensible, Scriptural, and untainted by evolutionary ideas. Hence this book.

Some illustrations have been disguised to avoid identification of persons involved. Much of the substance of the book has been delivered as lectures or sermons, and the method of direct address is in many cases retained. Pictures have purposely been left out because many good books offend by the nude pictures. For the ordinary person the book must not be technical, yet it must answer his questions intelligently and in an adequate and sufficiently scientific manner. Plain writing is needed, but healthy frankness must not provide material for morbid minds.

This book was written by a Christian minister with the help of medical practitioners, who gave suggestions and read the manuscript. The author also owes much to standard books. This book is for preventative purposes, in the field of mental hygiene. Dr. J. A. Rees, M.A., writes: "Over one third of the sickness in the civilized world can be traced to psychological origins."

There would be no need for sex education if the ordinary, everyday education of nursery and family life were functioning properly. The sex education of adults is essential if children are to be properly informed. Not everyone will be satisfied with the whole of this book. It is impossible on this theme to write such a book. Accept what you like; leave the rest, the next man may like it. Novels, films, plays of a certain kind, not to speak of "smutty yarns" that go around the places where we work, fling sex at us. In this sphere lie our greatest moral problems; our greatest temptations; whether we be married or not. Men and women have on their hands vast quantities of sex energy which will never be needed for biological purposes. How to handle this surplus is the problem. This book seeks to help in this direction.

PREFACE

ALLOW US to express our indebtedness to quite a number of persons; some writers, and an occasional lecturer, for ideals, thoughts, and scientific data which have been incorporated in the message of this "Manual of Sex Education."

The writer has feelings akin to Charles Lamb. He was approached as to where he received the inspiration for one of his effective essays. He remarked: "I milked some ten cows, but the butter I churned myself." Every author ought to give similar recognition.

The author has copyrighted this book, but he would be delighted to allow others to use any illustrations or subject matter in helping others with their sexual problems, which in these days are many and often very complex.

Should this book fall into the hands of those whose lives have been severely damaged by social vices and impurities, we point such to the Lord Jesus Christ for pardon, cleansing and transformation. Primarily, the book was written to aid in avoiding the pitfalls.

The object of this book is to give a lift for the things worth while. It is not so much our object to mark out the dangers, or tell frightening stories, but to mark out sane and safe paths. "If you have been upon these waters twenty-five years," said a young man to the captain of a steamer, "you must know every rock and sandbank in the river." "No, I don't," was the reply, "but I know where the 'deep water' is." That is the better course.

It is our fond hope that the book may counteract to some extent the wrong conception of sex life, especially of the eight million people most of them under twenty-one—who buy copies of some 150 nationally distributed periodicals reeking with frankly objectionable material. God says: "My people are destroyed for lack of knowledge."

It has been well said: "God placed within the body, enthroned in the nerves and tissues, and enshrined in the emotions of youths and maidens, an inward urge that impels to seek each other in full companionship. This we call 'love.' Bound up with this inner urge is the other part we call 'sex.'" Sex apart from real love is repulsive and alone tends to the sensual.

The sex question is related to our entire lives. It has to do with the body, the mind, the soul here and destiny hereafter. It has to do with every relation, every act of our complex lives. Millions of young people are swept into the deeper depths of passion's sea and never reach a safe harbor. The greatest problem of the age is proper sex control and relationships.

C. F. Derstine

Kitchener, Ontario, Canada

CONTENTS

PART I

SHOULD THE STORY OF LIFE BE TOLD?

CHAPTER 1

THE CRIME OF SILENCE

FORMERLY IT was considered unwise and indecent to discuss sex and related problems. It was thought that modesty demanded silence. Youth through this criminal silence sailed the high seas of life with all its dangers and was shipwrecked with appalling frequency. This false modesty and prudery led to much suffering among innocent women and children, caused by sex diseases and many tragedies in marriage.

Later, it was discovered that the sex functions were intimately connected with the physical, mental, moral and spiritual development of the individual and with the welfare of the entire race. People were learning that the clean, proper understanding and the right use of sexual powers were a sure basis of health, happiness and usefulness, and that these powers led to nobility, purity and health. It was felt that sex education would remedy many ills of the race.

Today, following this new awakening and discussion of sex matters, the pendulum has swung from silence to publicity that is almost nauseating. Literature, the stage, the newspapers and the movies have exploited the

15

universal interest in the subject. Altogether too often they have befouled the theme. The endeavor to get away from the false modesty of former years may end in the breakdown of the barriers of real modesty. The objective of this book is to find a middle-of-the-road course in the interest of social purity.

Alfred Tennyson wrote: "Self-reverence, self-knowledge, self-control; these three alone lead to sovereign power." All information should have this triune intent.

Ignorant children and inexperienced youth confront the vile and immoral things of the times. The base pictures, the smutty talk, the vile playmate, the questionable book and what not, come their way. Parents are youth's first line of guardians and defenders. Churches, schools, the State and interested individuals also share some responsibility to enlighten children and youth with vital facts.

If all the blighted lives caused by foolish prudery and criminal silence could speak, the voices would awaken millions by their thunderous tones. If all the terrible suffering and wreckage could be seen, the painful and humiliating experiences could speak, the sad tales told into doctors' ears could become known, the sights beheld which are seen on the operating tables of the world's hospitals, the confessions heard that have been made to ministers and priests alike, and the private records of the courts of the nation unlocked, it would not be difficult for parents to speak to their children. It would be a lesson that none could forget; important knowledge would be imparted and that before the life had been corrupted.

Parents ought to teach children the beautiful meaning of sex before vulgar jokes and distorted misinformation mar their lives. This confidence will tighten the bonds between parent and child. Often in deep soul anguish these words are spoken: "Oh, why did not my parents tell me the truth about myself? Why did they not sound the danger signal before it was too late?"

An American Judge Speaks

A prominent American judge says: "Nearly fifteen years in the Juvenile Court convinces me that there is hardly one child out of one hundred who has reached the age of twelve that hasn't come in contact with some sort of sex experience, either through vulgar stories or that sort of curiosity that is more or less natural and to be expected of a growing child. I used to think this was true of boys; but I am convinced—as is also the lady assistant judge of this court (who has sat with me in girls' cases for more than ten years)— that it is almost universally true of girls. We are almost constantly having to shock mothers with disclosures concerning the sex immorality of their daughters because of the cases that have come under the observation of the officers of the Juvenile Court." This should arouse parents to give proper sex instruction—an instruction to neutralize and offset the luridly colored misinformation.

Nature herself does not tolerate ignorance on this matter; she forces knowledge regarding it. The insistent questions of children, the awakening passion, and the nature of created sex organs all demand explanation. Who shall give scientific facts, simply, freely, frankly imparted, at the right age, and with tact? There is only one answer—that is, *the parents* to whom God has entrusted the child.

Shall it be evasion, falsehoods, fables, lies or truth? Shall the story of life be frankly and truthfully told? If not, children will find out the truth sooner or later, and will think less of their parents for keeping them uninformed or deceived. To refuse to guide them in this all important problem is to fail them. If parents can make confidants of their children on this question, they will naturally come with other questions.

Another factor causing parents to be silent is that some feel it would mar the innocence of childhood to know facts concerning sex. When finely given, properly proportioned, rightly graded and tactfully explained, parents need have no fear. It can be so treated that later on children will regard a filthy reference or low joke in connection with it as they would an insulting jest regarding their own mother.

Sexual knowledge can be imparted with such an air of mystery and with such evasiveness that children feel there is something about sex to be ashamed of, something which needs concealing. This is harmful. To mislead with fables of "storks flying in the window," or, "angels bringing them from heaven," is doubly harmful. Knowledge given just ahead of sexual development does not develop a morbid imagination and unchaste thinking. The safest link in connecting young children with proper knowledge of sex is the mother. Men are often awkward in their language in speaking to little children. Children take what she says as a matter of course. It carries weight with them. Later on the father should take on the task with the boy.

A knowledge of sex is as essential as to know how to read, write, count, or to know language, history, mathematics, geography, science, mechanics or any other branch of learning. The sexual impulse is controlled in the lower animals by instinct; in man it is guided by reason and controlled by the will. The attitude towards the sex impulse will be determined largely by the instruction given. If wisely imparted, the virtue of the individual will at least be safeguarded. Often health, happiness, success, character and destiny depend on how this knowledge is given.

THE DOCTOR SPEAKS

The noted doctor, P. A. Morrow, stated: "Fully one half of all the physical ailments common to young men from fifteen to twenty-five years of age is due to a violation of sex." Dr. Pique, in his investigations of the asylums of one nation, found that 82 per cent of the cases of insanity among the females and 78 per cent among the males involved their sexual mechanism; and that early sex instruction would have prevented much of this insanity and in other cases would have postponed the mental break in many cases until later in life. Thus we have the physical and the mental reasons for imparting sex understanding. Towering far and above these are the moral and spiritual reasons.

It is natural for children to ask questions, and the desire to know about its birth is no evidence of the child's mental depravity, but an evidence of mental awakening. For the child not to ask about its origin is evidence that it has heard about its birth and is keeping the information from its parents, or that the child is mentally backward. Questions are *golden opportunities.* Three methods for answering the child's questions are available: evasion, falsehood or the truth.

Evasion resorts to shaming, ridiculing, scolding and chastening the child. Falsehoods are often told, such as: "Angels brought you"; "The stork brought you"; "The doctor brought you in a big satchel"; "You were fished out of a pond"; "We found you in a brush pile." A certain family had a perpetual brush pile for the annual trimmings from the orchard. The cows found their calves there. The sows found their pigs there. The mare found her colt there. Hens and turkey hens found their nests there. No wonder that same boy eagerly searched the brush pile for some six months. Children so taught discredit their parents' integrity, lose confidence in them, keep what sex information they get from them, search for other ways to get their information which is often vulgar, and will later indulge in jests and jokes about the sacred function of sex and human birth.

Sex knowledge rightly given instills in the heart of the child respect for God and for His laws and a reverential awe for the wondrous miracle of the creation of their own lives. To be silent will be a thousand times more dangerous than to tell boys and girls the entire facts of their own sexual life and the miracle of reproduction. Ignorance does not make for purity.

Purity is in constant danger unless protected by knowledge which can safeguard it. Impurity is often the result of ignorance.

Light, knowledge and wisdom from God can clean up the foulest human cesspools. This is a child's right as a natural heritage. The sexual impulses are natural. With these impulses comes the call for facts. The Hebrew King Solomon in a lengthy chapter advises that this knowledge of sex should be imparted (Proverbs 7). Evil thrives on ignorance. The Prophet Hosea wrote: "My people are destroyed for lack of knowledge." May we not force youngsters to get their information from questionable sources; such as, impure associates, books and pictures which appeal to the vile and vicious in human nature.

SOMEBODY WILL TEACH

"Sex knowledge will be taught," said Mr. E. K. Mohr. *"If not in the homes and the Sunday school, it will be taught in the street."*

The writer feels that next to the home, the Christian Church and the Sunday schools are responsible for the Christian education of their youth. This should but supplement the teachings of the parents in the home.

The public school, the high school, the college, the university, the normal school and the Bible school and seminary should disseminate wholesome knowledge of sex and the methods of teaching the same to their students. However, this instruction must be given by clean-living, well-trained teachers, lest the instruction become a source of stimulation and the creator of the desire for improper conduct. The reverent atmosphere of *Christian institutions* makes them better fitted than secular institutions to bear this knowledge regarding personal purity.

Orison Sweet Marden tells the following gripping story: "I knew a mother in Washington, D. C., the wife of a man of national reputation, who had a most charming daughter, a girl of superb physical and mental endowment. Her great beauty and intellectual brilliancy attracted many admirers. The mother, like so many mothers, did not realize the dangers that confront young girls who are reared in utter ignorance of their sex nature, and never talked with her daughter on this vital question. She herself had been reared in the same way. The mother was easy and indulgent, and her daughter, as she approached womanhood, became spoiled by the attentions of men who flattered her beauty and brilliancy. Self-willed and headstrong, she drifted absolutely beyond her mother's control. Ultimately, the girl went on the stage, where she was especially exposed to temptations.

"Being utterly ignorant of her sex nature and the dangers and pitfalls that surrounded her, the girl very soon fell a victim to unprincipled men who hunted her as hounds hunt a deer. She got in with a fast set of people, learned to smoke cigarettes and drink cocktails, and in a short time formed other vicious habits. Though a brilliant actress, she ultimately lost her grip upon her popularity on the stage and deteriorated so frightfully that she passed away in an inebriate and drug asylum, a victim of the cruel conspiracy of silence upon the sex question. She was wrecked in the bloom of womanhood; she broke her mother's heart and nearly ruined her father's career."

"I would rather have the risks which come from free discussion of sex than the great risks we run by a conspiracy of silence," said the Archbishop of Canterbury (1930).

In Dr. Hamilton's *Research in Marriage* it was found that children wholesomely and naturally instructed by their parents at a very early age had more satisfactory married lives than those who received information later, often from unwholesome sources.

Dr. Stanley Hall, the great psychologist, writes: "My entire youth from six to eighteen was made miserable from lack of knowledge that anyone who knew anything of the nature of puberty might have given. This long sense of defect, dread of operation, shame and worry has left an indelible mark."

Dr. Exner gives an analysis from the answers of 948 college men to a questionnaire. From this we learn that 91.5 per cent of these men obtained their information from unwholesome sources. Only 4 per cent received it from their parents.

There are no practical books for small children; it is best told by the parents. It is unwise to send them to books. The mother should cease discussing sex with the boy when he approaches puberty.

Another reason many think of sex in the "hush-hush" style is because of urinal association; they feel these functions are "dirty." But it is not more so than any other part of the body.

The passing of the "Victorian" taboos will not ultimately prove an advantage unless replaced by clean knowledge, and a moral standard based firmly on the facts of the case.

An enrichment of life is possible, for which the sex element was intended in life, when we have left behind us the fears, false shames and embarrassments which have beset us.

A specialist of Wimpole Street, London, writes: "We should most of us agree nowadays that the child has got to have his questions answered when he asks them; that they must be answered truthfully, and that he should not be told more than he asks. The child who is taught in this way will know that he can always go to his informant when he wants more knowledge, and that he will always get a true answer."

Sir William Joynson Hicks, Home Secretary, London, England, said, when approached on the subject of indecent literature, by the London Public Morality Council: "If you will only in your churches, chapels, pulpits and Sunday schools, deal with the matter openly and frankly, and get the parents to realize it is their duty to do their utmost to keep these things [indecent sex appeals] out of reach of our young children and get the pure tone to the minds of the children, you will do more than I can."

PART II

HOW TO TELL THE STORY OF LIFE

FOR CHILDREN FROM FIVE TO EIGHT YEARS OLD

CHAPTER II

THE SIMPLEST ANSWER

THE FIRST QUESTION IS: "When shall I tell my child the story of life?" Sex education should begin in the home not later than the time when the child asks the first question about the origin of life. It should begin in easy, progressive stages, a little here and a little there, on through the years, until the child has become an adult.

A wholesome curiosity about birth and sex exists in all normal children. It is implanted by nature. It is a divine forethought. This interest generally shows itself at the age of five, six or seven years.

When a little child first asks, "Where did the baby come from?" or "Where did I come from?" or "Where did the kittens come from?" the mother's *golden opportunity* has come. The crucial hour has struck. To evade or resort to falsehoods can be disastrous. When the child discovers it has been deceived, it will not return to the mother for more information. It will go elsewhere.

Parents, both mother and father, ought to be prepared for what has been defined as, "four situations:

27

(1) The little child may ask some such question as is indicated above, that is, 'Where did baby come from?' (2) He may ask some utterly unexpected question, for example, 'What does it mean, half shepherd and half St. Bernard?' (3) He may ask some question beyond his years—some question the answer to which he is too young to understand. (4) He may *not* ask any question at all; either he has had his curiosity satisfied from other sources, or because he has got the idea in some way that it is improper to mention matters of sex."

When the child asks about the origin of his baby brother, or sister, he is often satisfied for quite some time with the simple reply, "He was born." The dread of many parents is the next question. What if he asks, "What does it mean to be born?" If he does, it is an indication that he is mentally ready for the next answer, "They come out of their mothers." Eventually, he may want to know more. A brief, truthful, unembarrassed answer will take care of the question, and the mother need not go beyond it. It will be accepted with equal authority as though it had come from the lips of a world-renowned medical man, or were the last words from the *Encyclopedia Britannica*.

In the event a child asks questions too unexpectedly for a ready answer, it may be necessary to postpone the reply. Geometry is not taught to first graders, but they do study elementary arithmetic. As much common sense should be used in a program of sex education. It is *not* wise to tell the whole story, unabridged, in answer to the first question. The child should be told some facts, and then informed that when the child is a little older, the rest will be told. The child's confidence by frankness should be kept, and *the line of communication kept open.* It is best to use the simplest language. This can safely be done.

*   *   *

AN AMERICAN DOCTOR WRITES:

"Just recently a young married couple came to my office inquiring about sexual problems. The lady made the statement that in her home they were never allowed to ask any questions about sex or where babies came from. She came from a very fine home, but this is a good index of many homes just like it. We breed youngsters in fatal ignorance. Children are always asking questions. We don't answer them, the church does not answer them, the State does not answer them, the school does not answer them, fathers and mothers do not answer them. But they do not go unanswered. They get answered. But they get answered wrongly instead of rightly. They get smudged instead of washed. They get answered blasphemously instead of reverently. They get answered so that the body is suspected instead of being respected. A boy who knows nothing asks a boy who knows nothing. A girl who knows nothing asks a girl who knows nothing."

*   *   *

CHAPTER III

THE FLOWERS

FLOWERS ARE beautiful, lovely and interesting. Children love flowers. Betimes, the best method of explanation for the little children is how flowers are born and grow. Some such way as this:

"Babies grow inside their mothers just as seeds in a flower. The seeds, when they are ripe, come out of the flower; babies, after they are big enough, come out of the mother's body and we say they are born." Sometimes it is good to point out that babies nest just under the heart of the mother. Because of this close connection physically she may point out the love and affection that a mother has for her little children.

This often will satisfy the child completely. Sometimes it may be desirable to show the child some simple flowers like the sweet pea and to continue somewhat as follows: "Do you see the fine, yellow dust in these flowers? It is called *pollen*. When the bee goes from flower to flower, it often carries pollen from one flower to another. The pollen contains the male cells. They go down through the slender tube in the center to the bottom part of the flowers, where they find the female

30

cells. There the male cells unite with the female cells. Then the new cells thus formed grow into seeds. We plant the seeds into the ground, and in the spring they develop into plants which bear flowers like these we are looking at. So in all kinds of animals and in people there are male cells and female cells, and both the mother and the father have a part in the development of the young." Thus curiosity is satisfied; the method of the Creator of all life is told at an age when no evil passions are aroused. All this is done before the ordinary story-teller of the street and school begins his sordid work. The child is forewarned and forearmed.

*   *   *

Nothing in life is more interesting, or more worth while, or more educational than to bring up a family of children."
            —James E. Peabody, M.A.

CHAPTER IV

THE NESTING BIRDS

THE CHILD may ask the mother: "Where was I when there wasn't any me?" Now it doesn't take much to satisfy the child's curiosity. Why deceive him? Why mystify him? Why not, in simple, chaste language, tell him the truth? The mother does not need to rob the child of its innocence. It can be done in a delicate way, without distressing him or her in the least. As the child gets older, give it more truth, but do not wait until it is too late. *Give most of the knowledge in advance of the sexual development.* The mother is the safest link in connecting young children with the whole mystery of sex. Nesting birds provide another approach which is normal and natural.

It is not necessary to tell many new facts at any one time. In the spring the child may be shown how the birds mate; how two of them are always together building the nest; how after a time the eggs are laid in the nest and the mother bird rests upon them with her warm body for a period of from ten to twenty days, leaving the nest and eggs only for a few moments to get necessary food; and how, at the end of the time, the young birds begin to hatch. The parent may explain how the mother bird continues to protect with her body, giving up, if necessary, her very life for the protection from enemies, until the birds are able to fly and to care for themselves. Where young chickens are raised, a similar explanation may be given.

Some children ask questions as early as four years or even younger; others, not until they are six and seven. If a child does not ask his parents of his origin before eight, it is wise to inquire. The child may have gotten his information from unsavory sources. It is always better to tell the story years too early than days too late. It is harder to *unteach untruths* than it is to *teach truth*.

*　　*　　*

"Anything relative to sex that can be taught a child before he is ten years old is just that much gain, for the topic can then be discussed with the utmost frankness, and with no self-consciousness on the part of the child."
—*N. Y. City Biology Teacher*

CHAPTER V

THE LITTLE PETS

CHILDREN ARE FOND of pets. Pets make good child educators. In the sphere of sex they strikingly bridge the chasm between parent and child. The pets may be the canary in the cage. The birth of a dog or the arrival of kittens contain beautiful sex lessons that can be taught children. In these instances can be seen the natural instinct for pairing and how this pairing in the lower forms of life foreshadows the home. All this should be wisely given, seldom very detailed, always with ample time between for the child wisely to assimilate past information given. If the questions of the child penetrate too far afield in the story of sex, it is possible to end the questions thus: "That is a good question. Sometime later, when I've given it my best consideration, I'll have another chat with you. But you understand, that is just between mother and her child."

Closely akin to pets are calves, lambs, and later in life, the young colts, all very impressive to children and youth.

Commend the child for having brought his questions to the parents. Compliments here go far. They pay good interest in increased confidence. Tell them that most of what they learned was taught them at home and that learning new things every day is the way children grow up to be men and women.

It is well to tell the child that after a while Mother will tell more fully of God's beautiful and wonderful plan of bringing children into the world. In school the child is given first a simple reader; then later on a more difficult one, and finally he can read and understand fully. First in sex education one should talk largely about things which small children can understand; as, seeds, flowers, birds, pets, animals; and then finally the last story. By the time the child is eight years old, he will be ready for the fuller story. Then as he grows older his parents will tell him more and more.

*   *   *

"Half-knowledge or perversion can warp the whole nature. Information gotten by subterranean channels often leaves an indelible stain on the soul."

—*An English Educator*

CHAPTER VI

THE STORY WELL TOLD

STORIES WELL TOLD have a universal appeal, especially to children. A prominent physician tells of one twentieth-century mother whose six-year-old boy was brought to her bedside and introduced to his two-day-old baby sister. She answered the boy's question as to where the baby came from in this way:

"Baby sister came out of Mamma's body; she was formed out of material taken out of Mamma's blood, and that's the reason Mamma's hands are so thin and white and Mamma's cheeks are so pale."

"Mamma, was I formed inside your body and formed out of your blood?" he asked next.

"Yes, my boy, you were, and that's the reason why Mamma loves her little boy so, because she gave her own lifeblood to make his body," the mother replied.

The little boy's eyes took on a faraway look, and he was evidently trying to grasp the great idea of mother-sacrifice. The writer says, "Evidently this child mind got at least a glimmer of the great truth, because presently his wide-open eyes filled with tears, and turning to his mamma he threw his arms about her neck and said, *'Oh, Mamma, I never loved you so much before.'*"

36

"In telling this wonderful truth in this matchlessly simple and beautiful way," writes the physician, "that mother made a new, strong bond between her own heart and the boy's heart that will hold them together in bonds of the strictest confidence and love throughout life. To this boy, parenthood is a sacred relation. That mother, by thus filling her child's mind with the thought of the sacredness of motherhood, completely occupied *the virgin soil,* giving no place for the noisome weeds of vulgarity and obscenity to germinate and grow. A child thus started in his knowledge of sex is saved from all that is vulgar and unwholesome for all that is pure and good."

*   *   *

PARENTAL RESPONSIBILITY

"Parents, don't think that your child is so innocent and does not think about such things. A child is born with sex and is sex-conscious from the time he is born. Recently several boys about nine or ten years old were walking down the street and one was overheard to say, 'When I'm nineteen years old I'm going to get married." Their minds are very active and we must help them to keep pure. Warn them of the sin of masturbation. They often get the habit innocently. Both boys and girls must be warned. They look up to grown people, and want to be like them. Help them to find good associates. Instruct them in purity."

—An American Doctor

CHAPTER VII

THE STORY AS THE MINISTER'S WIFE TOLD IT

DR. OSCAR LOWRY, in his excellent book, *A Virtuous Woman,* included the following well-told "Story of Life." This minister's wife, of the state of Iowa, determined that her children should receive their first knowledge of sex life from their parents. The two boys from that home, though full of life, vigor and fun, were different from most boys; their devotion to their mother was remarkable. Someone quizzed the mother as to the reason why. The story from her own lips follows:

"I have always told my boys the truth, for I made up my mind I would treat them like human beings, and, to the best of my ability, render them all the aid I could by giving them their first knowledge of the origin of life.

"One evening when alone, and soon after I knew a new babe was coming to live with us, I called them to my knees at twilight, as their father had gone to preach at a distant point. I breathed a silent prayer for assistance, for chaste, pure language in which to teach this sacred truth. In a low tone, and with a hand on each head, I said, 'My dear boys, Mother will talk to you about a sacred subject, so much so, that this must be a secret between Daddy, you and me.' Their faces were lifted up to mine, and I gazed into their clear eyes.

" 'In such a month, at about such a time, a little babe is coming to live with us, and be our own.'

" 'Oh, Mother! How do you know? Where is it now?'

" 'Listen, boys; when God created me, He made a little room right under Mother's heart. Baby is there now. When it is developed and when its limbs are large and strong enough, God will unlock the door, with much pain and suffering for Mother—but then we shall have this little treasure for ourselves. I shall not feel very well at any time; we cannot afford to have a hired girl; so you must be my helpers.' "

These two boys waited on their mother as though she were a queen; toiled until schooltime; and then hurried homeward at the close of the day. Once Walter timidly asked, "Will it be a brother or sister?"

"I do not know; that will be a surprise to me as well as you," she replied.

A few months later at eventide she struck the *golden opportunity* to confide something else to the boys. She opened the dresser, and there lay the garments which she had lovingly made. Together they looked them all over, decided which were the prettiest, and folded them away. Then one boy said, "We can hardly wait so long."

These boys did not discuss the matter with anyone. One evening, Bert, the oldest boy, came home greatly excited, his eyes flashing with anger.

"What is it, my son?"

"That fellow, a lad sixteen years old, made me so

angry as I was leaving the school grounds. Just as I was starting for home, he came and whispered in my ear, 'There is a kid coming to your home soon.' It made me mad to think of him calling our baby a kid."

The mother inquired as to what he said.

"Nothing, I just came home."

What a reward for that mother. How well that boy was protected from defilement by the instructions.

The mother said, "At last the long-looked-for event occurred. The happy father hastened upstairs to the boys' room the next morning, saying, 'Wake up, boys. Wake up; you can't guess what we have!'

" 'Yes, we can; we know; it's the baby! It's our baby, isn't it? Tell us quick.' "

Excited, they tumbled out of their bed, running joyfully downstairs to the mother's bedside. They went to meet not a stranger, not a new arrival only, but a new member of their own family.

Eagerly they greeted their mother with a good-morning kiss. They noted the paleness of her face because of the suffering of the night before. They quickly turned back the cover of the child's bed. Then they asked,

"Is it our brother or sister?"

"Your sister."

"Our little Ruth," and he sealed his remark with another kiss.

What a different world it would be if all mothers told the story of life in this spirit!

PART III

TELLING MORE OF THE STORY

FOR CHILDREN FROM NINE TO TWELVE YEARS OLD

CHAPTER VIII

FATHERS AND SONS

EITHER A father or mother, or both, may give the information in telling the story of life. Each has a distinct responsibility to both boys and girls. Usually the mother deals with the inquiring children until they are ten years old. The sex life is practically dormant until children are about ten years old. From this time on the boy looks upon life from the masculine point of view, and the father becomes the natural teacher. Wide-awake mothers will not cease rendering their share of good counsel. Children whose fathers are indifferent or who may not be living should be taught by their mothers the information that they need. She may secure books adapted to this age, or she may ask the family physician, his Sunday-school teacher, or his pastor to speak to him.

"It is a wise father that knows his own child," wrote Shakespeare. "I have noticed," said the late William Acton, M.R.C.S., "that the patients who have confessed to me that they practiced vice, lamented that they were not, when children, made aware of its consequences; and I have been pressed over and over again to urge on parents, guardians, schoolteachers and others interested

43

in the education of youth, the necessity of giving their charges some warning, some intimation of their danger. To parents and guardians I offer my earnest advice that they should by hearty sympathy and frank explanation, aid their charges in maintaining pure lives."

Fathers can give some advice to their daughters, which should be given from a man's point of view. Normally the girl after ten will go to her mother as a confidant and adviser.

The average boy's sexual instincts are probably at their height from fifteen to seventeen years old, and the sexual desires are then most insistent. In this period of grave peril, the youth needs the comradeship of a wise father. If the son can be kept from defilement until seventeen years old and if the mind is well fortified with healthy information, he will be comparatively safe thereafter. Altogether too many fathers feel that the mothers ought to do this task. This indeed is unfortunate. The father is better fitted.

It is strange that men who may nearly have been wrecked and who know the perils of sex and the risks in modern life do not warn their sons. A silent father makes the son think that he is ashamed to speak about the function which the Creator did not think it beneath Him to create in a marvelous manner. He may even think that the father's life may have been shady. When the son reaches the age of puberty, usually around thirteen years, the father should approach the son periodically, and have an informal chat with him. If the father begins early enough, this will be easy. Some young men in later years have expressed the idea that they often took long walks with their fathers in the hope that they would begin the discussion of this vital problem in their lives. Fathers should give them clean information. If this seems too difficult, the best possible literature in this field may be purchased and handed to the boy.

Fathers should assist their sons in getting the proper understanding of this divine instinct and in learning *the art of self-control.* The son should know that a life of vice leads to ill health and may lead to insanity and death; that vulgar men become sexual wrecks, often headed for the poorhouse; that they become nobodies, burned-out beings, on the road to a dismal failure.

Fathers should attempt to make their sons know that sexual forces, properly motivated, become the chief possessions of life—a good, healthy body, an active, trained mind, a fine, moral character, a splendid soul—all leading to a grand and noble success in life.

It should be impressed upon the boy's mind by the father that his whole future—his success, his happiness, his reputation and more—will depend upon a well-controlled life; that his own life, his future wife, his future family and posterity's well-being, are at stake; that clean living pays *here* and *hereafter;* that there is no lasting, permanent pleasure in vice; that *manhood* is better and easier kept than regained.

*   *   *

A great "Father of the Christian Church," some centuries ago, declared "that we should not be ashamed to speak of what God was not ashamed to create."

PRAYER FOR THE CHILDREN

Father, our children keep!
  We know not what is coming on the earth;
Beneath the shadow of Thy heavenly wing,
  Oh, keep them, keep them, Thou who gav'st them birth.

Father, draw nearer us!
  Draw firmer round us Thy protecting arm;
Oh, clasp our children closer to Thy side,
  Uninjured in the day of earth's alarm.

Them in Thy chambers hide!
  Oh, hide them and preserve them calm and safe,
When sin abounds and error flows abroad,
  And Satan tempts, and human passions chafe.

Oh, keep them undefiled!
  Unspotted from a tempting world of sin;
That, clothed in white, through the bright city gates,
  They may with us in triumph enter in.
                                —*Horatius Bonar*

CHAPTER IX

SAFEGUARDING READING, THINKING AND CONVERSATION

PARENTS AND TEACHERS should seek to safeguard youth in three common activities: *reading, thinking, conversation.* These are closely connected. The reading feeds the mind; the mind creates its thoughts; and from the mind flows the spoken word. The foundation of thinking and speaking is reading.

IMPURE READING

The bookstands are being increasingly stocked with vicious literature. This sex literature—trashy writing— is destructive to morality and to the spiritual well-being of youth. The low price brings it within the range of the pocketbook of the young. The lustful pictures arouse curiosity, and base desires are fed. The following actual account tells its own story effectively:

A young lady from one of the best homes in the central states approached the writer thus: "I don't know what is wrong, but I'm breaking down in every direction. Physically, I'm in bad shape. I can't think and concentrate on anything solid or worth while. I don't like to go to church anymore. I don't enjoy reading my

Bible as formerly. I've lost interest in teaching a girls' Sunday-school class, and they informed the superintendent that they want another teacher."

After she had answered a few questions, it was evident that questionable literature and the reading of putrid sex stories had caused the damage. The glow of a pure sexual life, which is a great boon to the individual and to those who come after, was almost gone because of the influence of sex stories with their undue stimulation of the imagination. The energies of the body were lowered, and the magnetism of the nervous forces was lessened. The mind and body are closely knit together. When the eye sees a well-laden table, the appetite is aroused and the digestive fluids in the mouth, such as saliva, begin to flow. So it is with the organs of sex. The mind that feeds on base sexual literature arouses a vicious circuit, which in the end taps the sexual organs of their product, throws it into the system as waste, and lowers the vitality of the body. She was told this and given some practical advice on how to attain the high ideal of *Social Purity*.

A year later a seemingly different girl with a new radiance in the face, sprightliness of step, and fresh interests, said: "Well I've made the grade; the trash was burned; new books were read; and I feel like a new person. Even the girls requested me to be their teacher again."

Impure Thinking

Thoughts are the seeds from which words and actions grow. Thoughts are the mainsprings of life. If the thoughts are unclean, then the words and actions will also be unclean.

> If we sow thoughts,
> We shall reap words and actions.
> If we sow words and actions,
> We shall reap habits.
> If we sow habits,
> We shall reap character.
> If we sow character,
> We shall reap destiny.

Purity is a health preserver, a youth preserver and a life preserver. The impure age rapidly. It is no mere figure of speech that *"Purity is power."* It is literally true. It is the chief requisite of lasting greatness.

If young persons poison their minds with vicious thoughts, it is difficult to turn around and still harder to restore physical soundness and soul purity. Unclean stories stick when placed in young minds. They are hard to forget. Hate them! Shun them! Shake them off as you would a viper.

Clean-mindedness cannot mean the absence of sexual thoughts. The presence of these thoughts by themselves does not defile. They are the common lot of all men. Dodge the "back alley rat" story-teller and the "smutty tale" bearer. You can't keep birds from flying over your houses; of course not. But you can keep them from making nests in your hair. "Wherewithal shall a young man [or lady] cleanse his [her] way? by taking heed thereto according to thy word" (Psalm 119:9). The prayer of King David helps: *"Create in me a clean heart, O God."* God CAN create a clean heart, and better still—He can keep it clean.

IMPURE SPEECH

Unclean thinking damages largely only one individual. However, indirectly it besmirches others. The person who uses foul speech and the vendor of filthy stories are double criminals because other lives are marred and broken.

Thoughtless, brazen, painted, cigarette-smoking, cocktail-drinking persons are not apt to think and speak purely. The inner life usually runs true to outer form. The ratio of clean-mouthed girls exceeds that of boys, but the margin is constantly growing less.

Young girls need to be on guard against older women who are purveyors of filthy talk. Age is impressive, and youth is impressionable. Girls are confidential to the writer's wife when she addresses women and girls, and they have repeatedly revealed the unfortunate fact that their minds have been soiled and their speech made indecent by the foul speech of older women. Guard what you *read* and what you *hear,* and your speech will be pure and clean.

It is no wonder that a Canadian lecturer to boys said: "Next summer when you expect to have a delightful time on your beautiful lake, rowing, canoeing, and picnicking—oh, yes, swimming, too—don't let some fellow come around to the 'old swimming 'ole' telling smutty stories and swearing. I want you clean boys to yell at him at once: 'Quiet there—put a cork into your mouth.' Ten chances to one he'll turn around and say: 'What's the difference? There are no girls around here!' Then you clean boys, you gentlemen, you'll just get furious, and retort: 'No, there are no girls around here, but there are some gentlemen. We want you to understand that! We don't allow rotten talk like that around here!' Say, boys, does the head wag the tail, or the tail the head? Why, the head wags the tail. Then which should clean boys be at the swimming hole—the head or the tail? Which should boss the swimming pool, the clean boys or the unclean?" That was well put to those high-school and grade-school lads. Should we not have the same attitude in all of our lives in every place we find ourselves?

*   *   *

BIBLICAL IDEALS

The words of I Tim. 5:22, "Keep thyself pure," augmented by Phil. 4:8, "Whatsoever things are true, whatsoever things are honest, whatsoever things are just, whatsoever things are pure, whatsoever things are lovely, whatsoever things are of good report; if there be any virtue, and if there be any praise, think on these things," should be the high ideal of every young man and young woman.

CHAPTER X

THE LIVING TEMPLE

THE NOTED and much beloved lecturer to boys and girls in Canada, Dr. Arthur W. Bealle, M.A., presented me with a copy of his chief lecture, *The Living Temple.* In it he tells the boys and girls the story of life in his own inimitable way. To encourage parents, he says: "Scatter diligently in susceptible minds the germs of the good and the beautiful; they will develop there into trees, bud, bloom, and bear the golden fruit of Paradise." He told the story of life clearly, plainly and convincingly thus:

"May I have your attention. Out of thousands of boys and girls I have met in the Province of Ontario, I have met only a few who did not know how to act like ladies and gentlemen. I have found only seven— just think of it—only seven boys who did not act like gentlemen. I know I shall not find the eighth in this school.

"I know you boys and girls are wondering and wondering why in the world that man has come to our school. He doesn't look like a school inspector and certainly not like a minister. I'll tell you exactly why

52

I've come to your school. I've come to make you
T-H-I-N-K. To think good and hard. How old will you
be in twenty years from now? You will then be a man
or a woman. What kind of man or woman are you
going to be twenty years from now? You said, 'Good.'
I'd rather be better than good.

"Someday, little by little, I hope you will climb the
dizzy heights and become better even than the best,
the 'cream of the cream,' as the French say—A-1.

"Here, now, at the top of the blackboard let us
write A-1. Canada expects me to be an A-1 boy; an
A-1 man; an A-1 husband; an A-1 father; and an A-1
citizen. You girls the same: an A-1 girl; an A-1 woman;
an A-1 wife; an A-1 mother; an A-1 citizen; then we'll
have an A-1 nation. That's doing the best for the nation. Someday you will be 'king' in the home, and you
will be 'queen' in the home. But to make good you
must do your part. To do your part you must know
that your body is a *Living Temple,* and Jesus Christ
must be on the throne."

The above is only an abbreviated form of the intro-
duction to the lecture. After it was delivered, he gave
every boy and girl a beautiful souvenir. It contained
much valuable information. On it was a place for the
signature where, he said, the child could write his name.
He called it their *Red Letter Day* when they signed it.
He said: "Keep it, and give it to your grandson someday." The souvenir magnified the body as the *Living
Temple,* speaking of it as a magnificent and a match-
less mechanism which must be kept fit and clean for
its tenants—the occupant and his God. The body with

its living soul is God's masterpiece, the climax of His glory, the acme of the splendor of God, and the epitome of the wisdom of God. This body must never be degraded, marred, debased, defiled, desecrated, dishonored, nor injured, but must ever be kept fit for the Holy Spirit of God. This temple is ten thousand times more beautiful and more sacred than all the temples and cathedrals of the world. There is only one kind of people that God lets into heaven; they are clean people —only CLEAN. Heaven is a pure place for pure people.

Following the general lectures to both sexes and the giving of the souvenir, Dr. Bealle delivered addresses to the boys and girls separately. During these addresses he told this story which is given here for the use of mothers:

"I visited a railroad town in New Ontario. One of the teachers, a real gentleman, met me at the depot. Very soon he said to me, 'Dr. Bealle, I am sorry you came to our school today!' Naturally, I sought an explanation. He exclaimed, 'Something very sad happened this morning. Last night Mrs. B—— had a little baby, and this morning she died!' Tell me, boys, did the people laugh, giggle, and tell dirty stories just because a baby was born and a mother died? Indeed, they did not. They all felt bad. But do you boys know what really happened?

"Let me tell you. That mother came to the edge of the grave. Then she slipped down, down, into the grave. Into a grave she did not want to enter so early in life. She died. The baby lived. How much did that baby's life cost? Why, the mother's life, of course.

The mother's life went out—the baby's life came in. Life for life.

"But do you boys know that your mother went into the same place of danger when you were born? She, too, almost went into the grave—ALMOST. Her tones were but whispers at last. She may have nearly fainted away, and asked, 'Where am I?' Your grandmother or some other lady was there, too, picked you up—*you,* a beautiful baby, fresh from the hands of God—and put you right into your mother's arms; your mother had never seen you before. Now when your mother saw you the first time, she did not tell smutty stories. You know well she didn't. She clasped you to her bosom, saying, 'How I love you.' She was thrilled. Why did I tell you this story about your being born? So that when street boys talk about mothers, babies, and being born, that you will remember the risk your mother took; how she suffered and brought you into this big beautiful world, and so you won't allow them to speak about it in an ugly way. You understand? Yes, I know you do. Thank you, boys."

THE POET AND HIS MOTHER

She loved me before I was born,
She took God's hand in hers and walked through the
    valley of shadows that I might live.
She bathed me when I was helpless,
She clothed me when I was naked,
She gave me warm food when I was hungry,
She rocked me to sleep when I was weary,
She held my hand when I learned to walk,
She nursed me when I was sick,
She suffered with my sorrow,

She laughed with my joy,
She glowed with my triumph,
When I knelt at her knee, she taught my lips to pray,
Through all the days of youth she gave strength in my weakness, courage in my despair.
She was loyal when others failed,
She was my friend when other friends were gone,
She loved me when I was unlovely, and led me into man's estate to walk triumphant on the King's Highway and play a manly part.
Though I lay down my life for her, I can never pay the debt I owe my Mother.

—Author Unknown

*   *   *

MY GOAL IN SEX DISCUSSIONS

"(1) A clean and wholesome view of the whole process of reproduction; (2) A love and consideration for his mother such as he never had before; (3) A chivalrous feeling towards every girl; (4) A firm resolve, if possible, never again to practice self-abuse, for his own sake, for the sake of the girl who will later be his life mate, and for the sake of the children who will call him father; (5) Such a loathing of venereal disease that he will be kept in time of temptation from any possible yielding to contamination."

—James E. Peabody, M.A.

PART IV

TELLING THE WHOLE STORY

FOR ADOLESCENTS FROM THIRTEEN TO TWENTY-FIVE
YEARS OLD

CHAPTER XI

THE DAWNING OF MANHOOD

IN THE LIFE of a boy the period of adolescence, which means becoming an adult, is both interesting and challenging. Boys want to become men in the true sense of the word. This change from boyhood to manhood occurs from about eleven to fourteen years of age. Since this change occurs in boyhood, every boy ought to know and understand to some extent at least what is taking place.

The responsibilities of men are different from those of women. Men's physical bodies are formed to work and to provide for their families; hence they need strong bodies. Women's bodies are formed to be homemakers, live indoors, and do the lighter tasks of life; hence they are not built so strong as men.

Besides the difference in the construction of the physical bodies of men and women, there is another marked distinction. Women are formed to give birth to children and to nourish them afterward. Men are formed to make possible the sperm cells, which when joined with the egg cells of the female, produce new children. This function of mankind is to wait until after the wedding day.

Before the time of marriage and the begetting of children, the boy's body develops into that of a man. This period of development is called puberty. The boy then gradually ceases to be a boy, and the dawning of manhood is at hand. During these days the voice lowers from a high-pitched boy's voice to the low tones of a man's voice. Hair begins to appear on parts of the body. He grows rapidly and at times exhibits unusual awkwardness.

In the male of the human being the sexual organs are located on the outside of the body. One of these organs is the penis, an organ that serves two purposes. Through this organ urine passes from the body and through it the sperm cells leave the body. Another of the sex organs is the testicles, which produce the sperm cell. The testicles are enclosed in a loose sac called the scrotum, which hangs back of the penis. In the testicles is stored a folded-up tube about twenty-five feet long. Near by are the prostate glands and Cowper's glands, which manufacture the fluid called semen, a thin milky substance containing sperm cells. Part of this semen is stored in two sacs called seminal vesicles.

The Creator in His marvelous design provided an internal outlet for the fluids from the sex organs during the days of early manhood. An additional substance, endocrine fluid, is a feeder to the nervous system and creates muscular and physical strength as well as helps to beautify the body. Some of this fluid passes directly into the blood, but if it is wasted, an aimless, shiftless, purposeless, stunted, dwarfed, unambitious specimen of humanity is the result. This internal secretion, if properly conserved, increases the powers of the mind and makes possible a magnetic life. Indirectly it makes for fine character.

Another factor which the adolescent boy should know is the provision which the Creator has made for excess semen. The overflow of this fluid occurs at different times, usually during the night. It is called seminal emission; some call these emissions "wet dreams"; others, nocturnal emissions. One should not worry over these occurrences.

Growing sexual powers need to be controlled. Later in life in the marriage state, you, as a man, will have the privilege of bringing into existence children of your own. This thrill will more than recompense you for having lived a clean, wholesome, self-controlled sex life. To achieve the mastery of sex control is God's challenge to man and woman which can lead to great spiritual heights.

*   *   *

SEXOLOGY

"Sexual science—sexology, as some would call it—differs, from many other arts in that it has no definitely circumscribed frontiers. From its center radiate beams into the whole range of human life, the spirit, the mind and the body. Sex penetrates the whole person."

CHAPTER XII

THE DAWNING OF WOMANHOOD

THE PERIOD when a girl changes into a woman is called the dawning of womanhood. The period ranges from the ages of ten to fourteen years, the average being about twelve or thirteen years. Every girl approaching this critical and important period of life ought to be informed on what is taking place in herself.

A number of outward physical changes take place. The enlargement of the breasts begins and continues to maturity. Later in life, if she be with child, her breasts will fill with milk for nourishing the infant. The arms and limbs develop and the hips grow broader to allow space for the unborn child and room for it to be born. Hair appears on several parts of the body.

Inside the girl's body there are marked changes during this period. The reproductive organs develop. Earlier they functioned by assisting the body, the nervous system, the blood stream, and developed the body into the balanced form of a woman. One organ is the ovaries which produce cells and eggs. Eggs fertilized by the male develop into babies. This fertilization is possible only by sexual relations with the male. Another reproductive organ near by is the uterus, sometimes called the womb. In the womb the fertilized egg develops into a baby. The womb is a hollow sac made of muscles.

Once about each month an egg leaves the ovaries, travels through the Fallopian tubes, and in about eight days reaches the uterus. If this egg is met by a sperm cell from the male, the egg is fertilized, passes into the uterus, and then attaches itself to the inner lining of the uterus where the formation of the baby begins.

Unfertilized eggs merely pass out of the body, most of them never becoming fertilized. To receive these eggs the uterus is prepared with an extra supply of blood and lining ready to hold the egg if it should become fertilized. This condition lasts for about ten days. Consequently, unless pregnancy exists, all this blood and fragments of the lining must leave the body by the passage called the vagina. This normal function is called *menstruation*.

This flow occurs once about every twenty-eight days, lasts from three to five days, continues as a rule from between the ages of ten and fourteen years until forty-five to fifty years. It is frequently called "the monthly period" or just "the period." The periods are not always regular in the beginning. Teamwork needs to be learned even by this delicate mechanism. The lapse in menstruation may be from January to June or menstruation may occur twice in one month. This may not be serious in early adolescent days, but in case of persistent unevenness, a physician should be consulted.

In time the periods should take on regular form and time. Preparations can then be made quite easily for sanitary protection. Formerly girls and women practically made invalids of themselves during these days, but physicians today advise reasonable carefulness. Exercise should be cautiously regulated by moderation.

Physicians declare that pain during menstruation is not necessary. When cramps occur due to over-abundance of blood in the blood vessels of the uterus, warm drinks, hot-water bottles and rest may relieve the pains. If not, the family doctor should be consulted.

This normal period need cause no alarm. The design of the Creator is accomplished during these days. Apart from this preparation for the continuance of human life, all life would cease on the earth. The transition from girlhood to womanhood is a normal change.

*   *   *

CHASTITY

"One of the most important matters that come to a young man and woman in their whole lifetime is the attitude toward chastity. This is why parents should seek to keep before young people all the scientific, moral, spiritual and historical arguments for chastity, to strengthen their normal resistance, to fortify them against the laxness they are aware of all about them."

Chapter XIII

MASTURBATION

Both fathers and mothers ought to understand the sexual problems of children and young people and realize the dangers of masturbation. This section of the book may be read to either boys or girls, or parts of it brought to their attention. Quite as early as the dangers of self-abuse can be understood by the child, it is advisable to give some information and warning so that the child is informed before vicious playmates influence their thinking in an evil way.

The Boy and Youth

A boy turns the corner to become a man at the age of twelve, sometimes at fourteen, usually at thirteen. At that time a mustache begins to appear; the voice breaks; hair grows at various places; he becomes awkward; and most important of all, he grows rapidly until he is about eighteen. This period, between thirteen and eighteen years of age, is a boy's hardest fight in his life.

During these days the sexual organs, sometimes called life glands (this term is used to simplify scientific terms for boys) create a powerful fluid. Scientists call this

65

fluid, semen, which is made by the testicles. This is the first function of the reproductive organs. Another substance is made which when conserved will make a broad-shouldered, strong, active man out of the boy. This production is called endocrine fluid. This fluid has nothing to do with reproduction. The life glands are never idle from childhood all through life. Day or night, whether awake or asleep, they generate energy which, if not wasted through self-abuse or other forms of sexual excesses, is distributed throughout the entire body. Consequently, this fluid can be kept for the body, or it can be removed artificially. This artificial removal medical men call *masturbation*.

THE GIRL AND MAIDEN

The girl turns the corner to bloom into young womanhood at the age of twelve years, sometimes at fourteen, usually at thirteen. At that time there is an enlargement of the breasts, a storing up of energy for future motherhood, which accounts for the charm and softness of the feminine form, and the growth of hair at various places on the body. A slight awkwardness is noticeable; the body grows rapidly; new emotions and impulses arise; strange moods and romantic longings are general. The girl becomes a mystery to herself. The meaning of all this is that sexual maturity is dawning, the age of puberty has arrived. This period is a girl's hardest battle.

During these days the sexual organs, sometimes called life glands (this term is used to simplify scientific terms for girls), secrete a powerful fluid. In every normal human being two essential materials are generated by these glands—germ cells and endocrine fluid. The former have to do with reproduction of life; the latter does not have. The glands are never idle from the dawning of puberty to the end of life, day or night. They generate an energy which, if not wasted through self-abuse, or any other form of sexual excess, is distributed through the body during the woman's entire lifetime. This secretion puts the radiance on the face of the girl, the energy into the mature lady, and the glory on the face of the aged lady. Consequently this secretion can be kept in the body, or it can be removed artificially by solitary vice. This removal medical men call *masturbation*.

EITHER SEX

Every person has more than a dozen secretion glands. The tear glands secrete a fluid called tears; the saliva glands, saliva; the sweat glands, sweat; the liver glands, bile; and the life glands, life fluid. Each when acting properly preserves health and makes living possible. If disturbed, ill health, and sometimes death, results.

The internal secretion produced by the sexual organs during life feeds the muscles and the nervous system, and makes for strength as well as beauty of the body. One of the products, endocrine fluid, passes directly into the blood. If wasted, it makes for an aimless, shiftless, purposeless, stunted, dwarfed, unambitious specimen of humanity. This internal secretion, if properly conserved, increases the powers of the mind, and makes possible a magnetic life. Indirectly, it makes for a fine character.

Nature has provided an outlet for the sex organs, a natural deposit into the blood stream. It is no more sinful to be conscious of sex desire than of hunger for food at dinnertime. Sex temptation is an indication of at least the possibility of rising to great spiritual heights.

Mature sex organs make it possible to propagate life. In marriage these organs are the instruments provided by the Creator so that human life can be continued on the earth. Without these organs the male does not become broad-shouldered, strong-muscled, and superbly built, nor the female beautiful. Domestic animals and fowl provide well-known proof.

This secretion contains living life cells, little bits of living matter. A million could be packed in a space the size of a pinhead. They may rightly be called a LIVING TREASURY. It contains the physical and mental inheritance of life from ancestor to ancestor and from generation to generation. This fluid is the work of a Master Mind. These germs cells have nothing to do with the body; they pass on family and racial traits. This Creative Mind planned well. A Master Chemist packed the characteristics of all living creatures into this life fluid. A superb Craftsman is He who created all the complicated sexual organs. No one understands all that constitutes sex, but the more we know, the more persuaded we can be that sex is not even in its physical aspects low or vile.

It is heritage to be well guarded. It should be passed down unharmed to the children, from generation to generation, until the end of time.

A prominent physician states: "Secret sin is the greatest curse to blossoming manhood. It takes the glow from the cheeks, and brightness from the eye and life-blood from the veins. Nothing so destroys the will power and vital energy; it weakens the intellect and impairs the memory. Such youths lose personal magnetism and attractiveness."

Dr. James Foster Scott says: "Masturbation in any form is exceedingly harmful in the injury done to both body and mind. Besides draining the system of vital fluid for gratification, it inflames the imagination and exaggerates the importance of the sexual function in the individual's view."

Dr. Snow gives the following testimony: "Self-pollution is undoubtedly one of the most common causes of ill health that can be found among the young men of the country."

Dr. J. H. Kellog says: "The physician rarely meets more forlorn objects than the victims of prolonged self-abuse."

Masturbation may be a slender cord, but later it becomes an iron chain of habit, to the dismay of many —a chain from which it is hard to free one's self. Feelings of guilt, shame, inferiority, self-loathing, horror, and above all, fear, do the chief damage in masturbation. It spoils the sacredness of the sexual relationship. The chief sin is the building up of lustful pictures. To continue masturbation one has to conjure unclean mental pictures. This breaks down self-control.

When these life glands are handled to produce a climax similar to that of intercourse the tender tissues are irritated and the muscles of the body are weakened. When tampered with so early, it produces a severe shock to the nervous system. The loss of the life fluid robs the blood stream of its richest secretion. If the practice is continued too long, it leads to physical weakness and ill health, nervous breakdown, mental dullness, and may end in severe mental disorders. Medically speaking—the chief damage is primarily temporary nervous exhaustion rather than the loss of semen.

*   *   *

SELF-RESPECT

"If ever parents had a duty to instill and teach self-respect, self-mastery and development to their children, it is today. Self-respect is the supreme court of individuality; it is the honest pride of trusteeship over self. Self-respect has a fine contempt for whatever is low and petty, mean and vulgar. It raises man to his loftiest level of living. It is not self-conceit. Self-conceit loves to strut. It is not self-esteem. Self-esteem tries to boast, or "blow its own horn." Such are self-love, while self-respect is insulated from all these. Self-respect has a certain reserve and a reverence for the fine dignity of the individual self."

—*Dr. G. D. Troyer*

CHAPTER XIV

TWO MAJOR SEX EVILS

YOUNG PEOPLE will never have definite convictions unless they have been adequately taught. No teaching of youth is well done unless it brings to their attention the two major evils of sex vice—fornication and adultery. Modern thinking tends to make light of these evils, but the terrible diseases which follow in their wake, the constant march of these victims of vice to hospitals, the crowding of insane asylums, and the cluttering of divorce court registers with cases of broken-down homes show their unchanging evil character. The voice of revelation (the Bible) still thunders its anathemas against these evils.

God's order for the reproduction of life is through the marriage of one man to one woman. Fornication is sexual intercourse between unmarried persons, hence an illicit or unlawful relation with the opposite sex. Fornication is rebellion against God's order.

Fornication is the enthronement of lust and the dethronement of reason. It abuses affections and robs the soul of its liberty; the flesh mounts the throne. It is the result of slavery to a rebellion of appetites and vile affections.

Fornication is a vicious crime because it leaves the mother without a legal husband, exposing her to shame. Then also it leaves the young child without a real father. In fornication it is plain that the man wants the sensual thrill, but refuses the consequences and responsibilities of marriage.

Motherhood ought to be a happy experience. To the unwedded girl it is a dire disaster, sullies the reputation, imposes disgrace on the unborn, and deprives her of the companionship of a husband at a time when she needs him most. Every youth should know that union of the bodies outside of wedlock is humiliating and immoral.

"If it were wise," writes Will Durant, "youth would cherish love beyond all things else, keeping body and soul clean for its coming, lengthening its days with months of betrothal, sanctioning it with a marriage of solemn ritual, making all things subordinate to it absolutely."

Adultery is the act of breaking the marriage vow of faithfulness. It is sexual intercourse by a married man with another than his wife or by a married woman with another than her husband. It is categorically prohibited in the Decalogue, by the seventh commandment: "Thou shalt not commit adultery" (Exodus 20:14). Adultery debases law, reason and order, and enthrones lust. It causes the breakdown of the family and nation. It is the cause of heartache to millions. It is a heinous crime. In Old Testament days, the penalty was death, and that by stoning. The New Testament declares that this sin can be committed by the eye and the heart.

Why discuss these evils? Because there is a dire transgression of the laws of God; there is an increase in illegitimate children. Increasing violations are everywhere evident between married and single folks, and an appalling self-justified attitude is taken by violators.

To put away a wife, or husband, save for the cause of adultery, is sin. To be the guilty party in a sexual relationship with a married person is a repulsive, improper expression of sex. Even though it brings its own train of remorse, the offender will have to face the judgment of God for his crime. Only repentance and faith in the Lord Jesus Christ's atoning death can cancel the guilt and only the Spirit of God can cleanse the heart.

Dr. A. T. Schofield, a Christian physician, London, England, points out: "There are more warnings against sexual impurity than any other sin, namely, eighty-two, that is, in the New Testament. The Old Testament is explicit in all things that relate to individual purity. Paul in every epistle speaks against sex immorality."

Sex expression outside of marriage is destructive of the best things. The Bible names such expressions as "adultery, fornication, uncleanness," and declares the penalty: "They which do such things shall not inherit the kingdom of God" (Galatians 5:21). "There shall in no wise enter into it any thing that defileth" (Revelation 21:27).

CHAPTER XV

KNOWLEDGE OF TWO MAJOR SEX DISEASES

FUNDAMENTALLY, SEX expresses itself through the body. It is imbedded in the physical body and is but one of the many functions of the body. Properly controlled and used, it ministers to our physical well-being, happiness and usefulness. The sexual organs can be a constructive force; they can also be a destructive force. Sex is one of the most powerful factors in life. The sexual instinct—next to self-preservation—is the strongest instinct of mankind. God has regulated this force by laws written in the Bible and in the body itself. It is God-ordained for the propagation of the human race (Genesis 1:27, 28).

The sexual endowment of mankind, when properly expressed, is constructive in the highest degree. However, when these laws are violated and vice is practiced rather than virtue, there is a penalty. The penalty is severe because the Creator endowed man with the powers of reproduction. Sex is the medium God uses in the propagation of human life. When nature is outraged, the results are weakness, mental dullness, insanity and vile diseases, such as syphilis, gonorrhea and related diseases. Infectious diseases also lie in wait for violators.

One of the major health problems confronting man-kind is presented by the two diseases, gonorrhea and syphilis, known as the venereal diseases, because they are usually transmitted by sexual intercourse. They may enter the body accidentally by contact with a diseased person. Syphilis ranks with the major diseases as a chief cause of death. Gonorrhea, according to the best authorities, does not often terminate fatally, but affects more people and often produces more distressing conditions in both sexes.

Syphilis is caused by a germ which can easily enter the body, sometimes through a break too small to be seen; it is also able to make its way through the broken tissues of the lips, eyes and genitals.

Gonorrhea, caused by a germ called the gonococcus, usually enters the body through the penis, sets up inflammation internally, mild at first, but later painful and accompanied by a discharge of pus. With women it is doubly serious because the reproductive organs are inside the body. This accounts for more deaths from this disease among women than among men. Both men and women need immediate medical attention in case of infection. This disease also seriously affects other organs of the body in many cases.

PAYING THE PRICE

According to William F. Snow: "In the final stages syphilis hardens arteries, causing a long train of ills by impaired circulation, large ulcers which if healed will leave ugly scars, sometimes resulting in the loss of the nose, which are cruelly disfiguring. The most tragic are the effects upon the brain and the spinal cord which often result in loss of the mind due to softening of the brain, in locomotor ataxia which slowly produces the loss of control of the legs and arms and other parts of the body, and cerebral hemorrhage or apoplexy."

The following generation from infected parents often pays the most in suffering. There are tragic possibilities for children. Many die before birth or before the first year by being infected by their parents. Others live on in defective bodies or minds, deaf or blind. Some by proper treatment are saved from these appalling effects.

With reasonable precaution and ordinary hygienic care in everyday life, the unmarried young man or woman, who refrains from physical intimacies, such as kissing, intercourse, and the like, is practically exempt from either disease.

The Creator bestowed on woman the most exalted privilege that He bestowed on any part of His creation—that the Son of God should be born of a woman, independent of man. Thus the female was made the highest human instrumentality in blessing the world.

When women and girls stoop to illicit sex relations for mere indulgence, become the temptresses of men, they fall from the summit to the lowest depths of life. All too soon this course leads to the hospital, the operating room, mental institutions and premature death.

Dr. P. A. Morrow, New York City, declared that at least seventy-five per cent of the operations on women are because of female troubles. A considerable number of these are caused by girls having had their so-called "fling," or by being married to questionable young men, who thought it would do no harm to sow their wild oats. Some "blooming brides" often become pale, confirmed invalids in a few months; they can age ten years in ten months. Many girls pay in later life by being deprived of the crowning privilege of the Queen of the Home, that is Motherhood, through the forced removal of ovaries and sometimes the womb as well.

Venereal diseases constitute one of the greatest of public health problems. The following facts as to venereal disease are issued by the Health League of Canada.

Syphilis has been called the great killer. Gonorrhea has been called the great sterilizer.

Syphilis is responsible for (1) many deaths — as a world problem it outranks all other infections as a cause of death; (2) insanity—syphilis is responsible for general paralysis of the insane, one of the most terrible of all forms of insanity; (3) locomotor ataxia; (4) aortic aneurism; (5) many cases of cerebral hemorrhage or apoplexy; (6) a very large proportion of operations, miscarriages and still births; (7) many infant deaths.

Syphilis, untreated, will cut life one third. In addition it will cause many types of disability which fill hospital and institutional beds in all parts of the country.

Gonorrhea is responsible for (1) a large proportion of major operations on women, for ailments peculiar to women; (2) 80 per cent of blindness in new-born infants; (3) thousands of abortions and miscarriages; (4) certain types of crippling arthritis; (5) certain types of sterility in both male and female. Many childless marriages are due to this cause.

These two diseases are a major public health problem. Their control depends to a large extent on public education calculated to inform people as to their seriousness, as to the fact that they are highly communicable and that they may be cured by regular treatment, especially if that treatment is instituted early.

ACTUAL CASES

Recently a young lady in her early teens under medical attention in the ward of a Canadian hospital was being treated for a venereal disease by nurses who wore long rubber gloves. She remarked to a patient in a near-by bed, "I wish they would treat me as nicely as they treat you." Poor girl! She did not know the highly contagious character of her disease and the seriousness of her own condition. She was paying for sex violation in her physical body.

Two instances must suffice: A young man is requested to stand on his feet in the operating room of a Kansas City Hospital Clinic. The operating surgeon points to his blackened sexual organs, prior to a major operation, in the presence of budding surgeons and doctors in training, and says, "This young man is paying for sowing his wild oats. This operation but removes the sexual organs, and may lengthen his life some six months." He paid a high price for wrongdoing.

A strong, healthy, robust young man, living near Lima, Ohio, went out for a so-called "good time" one Saturday night. He met a young lady of questionable morals. Through illicit relations with her he contracted a disease which in some eight months ended his life.

The county authorities erected a shack in the woods, where he was cared for by the county doctor and nurse till the end. One day he remarked to a dairyman friend of mine, "If only somebody had told me about such diseases, I would have behaved myself that night." Because of the lack of understanding this young man found out too late the meaning of the Biblical passage, Proverbs 7:21-27, which reads:

"With her much fair speech she caused him to yield, with the flattering of her lips she forced him. He goeth after her straightway, as an ox goeth to the slaughter, or as a fool to the correction of the stocks; till a dart strike through his liver; as a bird hasteth to the snare, and knoweth not that it is for his life. Hearken unto me now therefore, O ye children, and attend to the words of my mouth. Let not thine heart decline to her ways, go not astray in her paths. For she hath cast down many wounded: yea, many strong men have been slain by her. Her house is the way to hell, going down to the chambers of death."

With many, a venereal disease results in medical costs and the loss of wages. According to insurance company statistics, medical services cost some $184.01 per afflicted person. The cost in one American city alone is fifteen million dollars annually. Insurance tables reveal that those suffering from syphilis shorten their lives on an average of twenty-two and one-half years. They pay in money, misery, and in shortened lives robbed of happiness, health and character. Dr. P. A. Morrow said: "Fully one half of the ailments of young men are due to the violation of sex laws."

Every normal young man looks forward to marriage and a home; beyond this, to children, yea, posterity, a deposit of all of the finer things contained in his own life and that of his life companion—his wife.

Too often young men joke about love and marriage and forget all that it involves. Its chief involvement is the future generations. Taking chances endangers a young man's fitness to marry. Certain diseases make it possible for him not only to infect his wife but children for years afterward.

While the writer was lecturing in a prominent Illinois city, a pastor approached me with this difficult question: "What shall I tell this young man?" He continued, referring to the following words spoken by this young man: "I lived a reckless life; was infected by questionable relationship with women, then was called cured by the medical profession. Then I was married, and now my little daughter of seven years asked me these questions: 'Daddy, why do I have this running sore on my face? Why don't the little children play with me? Why can't I go to school and Sunday school like other girls?'" The young man with a sober face said to the pastor, "Will I be damned if I take the life of that little girl to get her out of her misery, and then take my own life afterward?" What a price! He asked those questions too late; he should have asked other questions earlier.

The American Social Hygiene Association estimates that five per cent of the American people have syphilis and ten per cent have gonorrhea.

THE PRICE HE PAID

By ELLA WHEELER WILCOX

I said I would have my fling,
  And do what a young man may;
And I didn't believe a thing
  That the parsons have to say.
I didn't believe in God
  That gives us blood like fire,
Then flings us into hell because
  We answer the call of desire.

And I said: "Religion is rot,
  And the laws of the world are nil;
For the bad man is he who is caught
  And cannot foot his bill.
And there is no place called hell;
  And heaven is only a truth,
When a man has his way with a maid,
  In the fresh keen hour of youth.

"And money can buy us grace,
  If it rings on the plate of the church;
And money can neatly erase,
  Each sign of a sinful smirch."
For I saw men everywhere,
  Hotfooting the road of vice;
And women and preachers smiled on them
  As long as they paid the price.

So I had my joy of life:
  I went the pace of the town;
And then I took me a wife,
  And started to settle down.
I had gold enough and to spare
  For all of the simple joys
That belong with a house and a home
  And a brood of girls and boys.

I married a girl with health
    And virtue and spotless fame.
I gave in exchange my wealth
    And a proud old family name.
And I gave her the love of a heart
    Grown sated and sick of sin!
My deal with the Devil was all cleaned up,
    And the last bill handed in.

She was going to bring me a child,
    And when in labor she cried,
With love and fear I was wild—
    But now I wish she had died,
For the son she bore me was blind
    And crippled and weak and sore!
And his mother was left a wreck.
    It was so she settled my score.

I said I must have my fling,
    And they knew the path I would go;
Yet no one told me a thing
    Of what I needed to know.
Folks talk too much of a soul
    From heavenly joys debarred—
And not enough of the babes unborn,
    By the sins of their fathers scarred.

CHAPTER XVI

THE SEX STORY SCIENTIFICALLY SET FORTH

TO BE A REAL DAD to a real boy or A REAL MOTHER to a real girl is the biggest task in the world. Experience proves this to be true. However, when the boy and girl stand at the threshold of manhood and womanhood, then it is that parents need to enjoy the esteem, confidences and fellowship of youth. During this transition period, powerful forces are at work within the physical body, the intellect and the inner personality. This calls for parents to be real pals to their children.

Mother usually make the best teachers to convey the important and delicate knowledge of sex until boys are ten years of age. Up to this time children are without sex consciousness. Frequently, fathers do a good supplementary job. If the mother is not living, or if she be careless, the father must either convey information or request a closely related mother or Christian physician to do it. From ten years upward the boy gravitates towards the masculine and responds better to knowledge given by the father.

This chapter of the book was written to enable the parent to tell the story of life directly, comprehensively and scientifically. This section may be read to the youth who has reached the age of puberty, or the whole book may be given the youth to read for himself or herself. Sex knowledge properly given cannot do them harm. Altogether too little may be given them, and that little too late. It is best to be on the scene before the purveyor of smutty sex stories begins his or her nefarious work. The story is told as follows:

As Christians accepting the Bible, we turn to the oldest account of the beginning of human life. This account has been endorsed by Jesus Christ when He said: "In the beginning God created man male and female." The beautiful Genesis account of the creation of human life has never been disproved.

Human life had its beginning when God created the first man, Adam, "the father of all the living." His life came directly through the creative powers of Almighty God. This body was marvelously designed and was the handiwork of a Master Architect.

Life is expressed through three mediums: the body, the mind and the spirit. The human body is a magnificent edifice for the habitation of the immortal human spirit. That same body is designed to be the *temple* of the Spirit of God.

Following the creation of man, God by His supernatural power created woman from an integral part of man. This partner of man was called woman, because she was "of the man" and became "the mother of all the living."

The wedding was performed by the Creator, and from

this sublime pair, fresh from the hand of God, sprang the whole human race.

To perpetuate the human race and to people the earth, God created them male and female. There is a distinct difference in their personalities and in their physical structure. Man is stronger and more rugged than the woman. The man is adapted to outdoor life; the woman to indoor life.

THE MEANING OF MALE

Besides the differences in physical structure and in personalities of men and women, there are differences in the sexual organs. Together they have the power to reproduce a life but the function of each is different.

Man is born with two exterior glands called testicles. One of the products of the testicles passes directly into the blood and is therefore called an internal secretion. This product is called body builders. No one knows its chemical formula. It is also called hormones (Greek for *exciter*) because it excites or causes changes in the development of the body. It is a body building product and profoundly affects the body. It is the chief factor that changes a boy into a man. Going through the arteries of the maturing boy, this secretion together with other internal secretions undertakes no less a task than that of gradually transforming him into a man. All human beings have two essential materials, body builders and germ or sperm cells. A similar process takes place within the female.

The second product of the testicles has to do with the reproduction of human life—the birth of children;

it is called sperm cells. These little sperm cells are so tiny that they can be seen only under the most powerful microscope. Scientists tell us that a million could be placed on the head of a pin. Their work is the reproducing of the human body. They are alive. They are the fertilizing agency which the Creator designed to continue human life. These germ cells contain an awesome and sublime power.

One of the secretions builds up bone, nerve, blood and flesh but can never launch a new life, for it is forever barred from creating new life. The other secretion has such powers and holds within itself the traits of our ancestors. It is the living treasury of the past handed down from ancestor to ancestor. Consequently the male can and does pregnate the female. This is the reason for the practice of morality which protects all life and calls for self-control of the reproductive powers until the right time for their use in the days after marriage, when the home is established.

THE MEANING OF FEMALE

The female has not only a lighter frame but a different personality from that of the male. She is constructed for a different purpose, that is, to be the mother of human beings who are to be born according to the laws of God.

The sex organs in the female are on the inside. Two ovaries which correspond to the testicles in the male are lodged safely within the abdominal cavity. They are thin, oblong glands, one and one-half inches long and about half as wide.

Female sex organs also secrete hormones, sometimes called body builders, which contain elements that build the body, create energy, make for magnetism, and even increase the powers of the mind. During single life and married life they are the woman's boon friend for general well-being.

These glands with their hormone secretion carry female germ cells from which an egg develops. Some four hundred of these eggs, scientists tell us, are formed in a woman's lifetime. Most of them will die. This large number is formed so as to make certain that the human race will continue to multiply as God commanded the race to do.

THE REPRODUCTION OF LIFE

Now for the answer to the question so constantly asked by children and youth: "How were we born?" Every step of the story of life is clean, wholesome, pure and worthy of the mind of a great Creator and Divine Master Mechanic. Here is the story:

Human babies are born within the mother. The beginning of life is the journey of a very, very small egg, smaller than the dot at the end of this sentence. This egg comes from the ovary. There are two ovaries in the body just below the waistline of the mother, one on each side. The journey is from the ovary to the uterus (womb) of the mother. Along this path, if the father and mother show their love and affection for each other and at the same time have sexual contact with each other, the egg of the female meets the sperm of the male. Under normal conditions at that moment it is possible for a life to be launched that will exist eternally.

If the sperm of the male meets the egg of the female, the two cells become one and form a new human life. This new cell fastens itself on the walls of the uterus (womb). In two months this new life will grow to the size of merely one inch. In two or three months more there will be movement to the extent that the mother can know the babe is alive. In nine months the baby will be full grown, and ready for life in our world.

To come into our world the uterus will contract powerfully producing pain. This contraction will enable the babe to leave the body of the mother. This pain is normal and should cause no alarm to the young husband and wife; it is called *travail*. This then is the birth of the child.

You probably have noticed and wondered about the raised mark on your abdomen called the navel. During the period of nine months inside the body of your mother all babes are joined at this navel point to their mother by a tube, called the *umbilical cord*. Through this tube the unborn child is nourished by the mother from her own blood stream. Later the babe is fed from the breasts of the mother, and later spoon-fed by the mother. Ultimately, the child feeds himself. This is the clean, pure, amazing, startling and sublime story of life. Sex is, and has always been, a beautiful and entirely natural thing. Happy is the person who counts nothing God has made—and He made the sex instinct— common or unclean.

PART V

THE STORY TOLD FOR PARENTS AND
TEACHERS

CHAPTER XVII

PREVENTION OR RESCUE LECTURES

AFTER A WRECK upon the rocks, a lifeboat of course is good, but a lighthouse to prevent a wreck is infinitely better. Prevention is always better than cure. *"Formation of life"* is better than reformation. A fence around the top of a cliff to prevent the unwary from tumbling over is infinitely more sure and advantageous than a thousand ambulances in the valley below even though the victims are promptly picked up.

Multitudes of young men and young women are ignorant of the perils to which their lack of wholesome knowledge and sex training exposes them. Later they are the victims of "wild oats" sowing, reaping a frightful harvest of untold mental and physical agonies as the result of such ignorance. Many young people enter life floundering through the swamps of misunderstanding, misinformation, doubt, perplexity and fear regarding sex.

We recognize the right of youth to have sex knowledge, for their health, happiness and spiritual well-being are dependent upon it. This knowledge cannot come too early if properly given in right proportions. Silence on this important theme is criminal. Too much so-called "information" is tainted. Often all that some inquiring youths receive is evasion, falsehoods, and no truth. There is a place for modesty, but none for prudery.

There is nothing about comradeship between the sexes, courtship, love, sex, homemaking and marriage which is not at once beautiful, thrilling, worth while, and worthy of the purposes of the Great Designer and Creator.

With so much at stake, why get information (misinformation) from schoolgirls, street urchins, foulmouthed sex purveyors, smutty sheets, movies, tainted literature, or other improper places? Dr. Garth Boeriche, Head of the Department of Therapeutics, Hahneman Medical College, Philadelphia, Pennsylvania, said to a class of young medical students: "Gentlemen, the benefits of a pure life are reaped after forty years, and vice versa, the evil effects of an impure life."

Consequently, life should be enlarged by self-knowledge, and can be greatly enriched by self-control. If life is motivated by an intelligent and spiritual self-expression, it will find the higher levels of human life. Those who find out these higher laws of God written in the Bible and the physical body, laws of "sex expression" in right directions, and who also obey these laws, are empowered in all spheres of life. Those who disobey them meet defeat and disaster.

The author believes in rescue work, believes in the preaching of the Gospel which brings salvation within the range of all men. It is possible to snatch a forlorn piece of human wreckage from the waves of vice, as brands from the burning, and it is possible to regenerate sin-marred men and fallen women. Nevertheless it is a thousandfold better to "train a child in the way it should go" so that when it is older it will walk in wisdom's ways. Training a child properly is primarily based on the giving of proper knowledge by trained parents and teachers.

There are few adults who are prepared to tell the story of life to the child and fewer still who are able to give the additional instruction as the child grows older. Nature will not teach parents, teachers or lecturers how to teach sex truth in a wholesome and efficient way. This, then, implies training.

Dr. T. H. Shannon points out that there are three indispensable qualifications needed by parents, teachers and lecturers. They are the following:

THE MORAL QUALIFICATION: They should regard the functions of sex as pure and sacred, and be accustomed to think and speak of sex in a reverent manner. Fathers who tell smutty stories are disqualified. Mothers that descend to shady insinuations have lost their influence. Teachers must have a clean record.

THE MENTAL QUALIFICATION: Parents, teachers and lecturers must at once command a clean sex vocabulary. (This book includes a wholesome sex vocabulary. See page 96.) Unfortunately, many grownups cannot speak of the organs of sex, their functions and abuse, without using the language of the street. This suggests impurity to the child, who associates this language with the use on the schoolground. Then, too, teachers must understand the functions of the sex organs and their close connection with life in general. This understanding is essential and one of the objectives of this book.

THE EFFICIENCY QUALIFICATION: Tact and skill are prime factors. It requires time, reading, thought, observation and personal experience to develop skill. Motives may be sincere, but the ability to present this knowledge is necessary lest it be told too bluntly, awkwardly, severely or too suggestively. Unwise handling of this topic may do more damage than good. Where parents feel that they do not possess this ability, it is best to give the child the proper books and also to read to the child, at the right time, from books such as this one. This is the secondary objective of this book. The first objective is to impart knowledge to the parent and teacher; second, to impart knowledge to the child and youth.

Parts of this book should be used and adapted to the age, sex and intelligence of the individuals taught. All instruction should be given in a dignified, manly, sober, sane and reverent manner and in the same way in which any other vital truth would be discussed.

Every church congregation should arrange for these lectures periodically. Communities and schools should do likewise. However, these lectures should be given by men that are experts and by men whose character is beyond reproach, the content of their messages being considered before they are engaged. This is very necessary because many lecturers on sex and books on sex are tainted with the virus of evolution and other questionable attitudes towards sex.

To do the best task there should be a series of

lectures: one to married men, one to married women, one to young men, one to young ladies, one to boys and one to girls only—six in all. These could be given nightly before the regular message to the mixed audiences.

Where such lectures have been given, there has been a marked improvement in moral living and social purity.

It is possible to give lectures to men and boys mixed, and to women and girls mixed, if advice to married folks is largely eliminated, not because advice to married folks is vulgar, but it is unnecessary if given too early.

* * *

WISE COUNSEL

"It is not in knowledge alone that there is self-protection amid the inevitable risks of life. Self-control and a deep sense of responsibility must go hand in hand. Mere instruction is insufficient; there must be a slow training of emotions in the face of the facts of life. We need wholesome surroundings, sound economic conditions, so that none need to be turned into the downward paths."

CHAPTER XVIII

A CLEAN SEX VOCABULARY

A CLEAN VOCABULARY is a prime requisite to clean thinking and living.

ADOLESCENCE*: The period in which boys and girls develop and grow into men and women.

AFTERBIRTH: The mass of membranes, etc., which comes out of the uterus after the birth of the child.

BIRTH*: The process of being born.

BIRTH CANAL: The vagina; the canal through which a baby passes out of the mother's body.

BREASTS*: Two glands on the chest of a woman which supply milk for the baby.

CAESAREAN BIRTH: Birth of a baby by special operation through abdominal walls.

CELL*: The smallest single particle of living matter.

CHILDBIRTH*: The actual birth of a baby.

CHROMOSOMES: Small bodies inside a cell, which carry the qualities that are inherited from parents and ancestors.

CIRCUMCISION: The act of cutting off the foreskin of the penis.

COITUS: Sometimes called sexual intercourse, the mating of male and female.

96

COWPER'S GLANDS: Two small glands which aid in the production of semen.

EGG: The female reproductive cell.

EMBRYO: The baby inside the mother the first three months.

FERTILIZATION: The union of the sperm cell of the male with the egg cell of the female.

FETUS: The baby inside the mother from the third to the ninth month.

LABOR: The contraction of the uterus that forces the baby out of the mother's body.

LABOR PAINS: The normal pains which accompany childbirth.

MENSTRUATION: The flow of blood from the uterus, about every 28 days.

OVARY: One of the two female organs in which the ova or egg cells are formed.

PENIS*: The male organ which discharges the urine.

PREGNANT: When a baby is developing in the female body.

PROSTATE GLANDS: A gland in the male which makes semen.

PUBERTY: The period in which boys and girls start to develop into men and women.

RECTUM*: The end of the large intestine.

REPRODUCTIVE ORGANS*: The organs of the male and female which take part in the process of reproduction.

SCROTUM*: The sac below the penis which contains the testicles.

SEMEN: The fluid by which the fertilization sperm is carried.

SEMINAL VESICLES: The two small sacs which store the unused semen.

SPERM: The reproductive cell of the male.

TESTICLES*: Two male reproductive organs which lie in the scrotal sac and produce the sperm cells.

UTERUS*: The womb; the organ which carries the unborn babe.

URINE*: The fluid secreted by the kidneys, cast off as waste.

VAGINA: The passage in the female leading out from the womb.

Words marked with a star (*) should be taught to boys and girls before the age of twelve; the other words afterwards.

CHAPTER XIX

REGAINING LOST MANHOOD AND WOMANHOOD

THIS BOOK MAY FALL into the hands of some readers too late to prevent the loss of ideals and degrading habits. The practice of impurity and indulgence of vice may already have debauched the imagination and enslaved the reader with evil habits. It is possible that some reader may have contracted vile diseases by indulging in the grosser evils of fornication and adultery.

The diseased should at once consult a reputable physician. Modern methods of treatment go far to stop the ravages of venereal diseases. No treatments will entirely remove the damage done, but they may save the sufferer from an untimely death as well as keep others from being infected by the disease. Such we would point to the Creator, their God, who has made provision for mercy and forgiveness through the Lord Jesus Christ. Not only forgiveness is possible, but the proffered gift of life eternal is at the disposal of the offender in spite of his wrongdoing. This new imparted life alone can give complete mastery to the fallen.

Both the grave offenders and the lesser offenders, who have violated the laws of God by self-indulgence in

99

secret vice, self pollution, known as masturbation, become the victims of quack doctors. Such men bleed the victim of his money and often leave him worse than they found him. These medical blackguards are out for the cash. They do not have the slightest regard for the welfare of their patient. They describe in lurid colors the symptoms of "lost manhood" and "lost womanhood." These so-called specialists call normal night emissions "losses" and "pollutions" in order to frighten their victims. They work so powerfully on youthful imagination that youth is constantly conscious of his state and watches for every symptom of "lost manhood," until the mind becomes unbalanced. This draws the victims to the quack's office.

If parents have children, teachers have pupils, or, if the reader has fallen into a life of vile and impure habits, we would advise them to read the last chapter of this book, "The Pathway to Noble Manhood and Beautiful Womanhood." Much of the counsel given to keep from the path of the destroyer will also help in getting away from his clutches.

The way back to purity may be hard, but there is a way back. Desire to be pure. Promise your God, that by His divine help you will be free from enslaving habits. Say it, and mean it: "I am going to conquer this habit which is destroying my vitality, sapping my life, and ruining my prospects. I am going to recover my self-respect, my manhood, at any cost. I am going to fight this thing to its death." There must be an act of the human will. It is written of that grand young man, Daniel: "He purposed in his heart that he would not defile himself."

My suffering young friend, your condition is not hopeless. The powers within your body have recuperative ability. Nature has curative forces at her disposal. Do not lose heart. Keep your mind wholesomely occupied in the better things of life. Read the best of literature, the most inspiring writings. Free the mind on sexual matters as much as possible. Work hard; play hard.

The secret of lasting recovery is not in some drugs, some quack remedies; it is you yourself, your mental determination to be true to the higher ideals of life.

Do not expect to reach the peak of recovery immediately. The roadway to purity, strong physical vitality, mental vigor and spiritual purity is not covered in a brief spurt. Downgrade traveling was not a matter of a day or weeks; so upgrade traveling will not be a matter of days and weeks. The decision to turn about may be a matter of a given moment, but the making of the grade takes time. Do not dally; the break with impurity *must* be instant. There is no such thing as gradually breaking away from the vice of impurity. It is recorded of the Prodigal Son, Luke 15: *"I will arise and go."* The decision was instantaneous, but the journey home took time.

The power of God, the forces of heaven, the inner resources of the human spirit are at the disposal of the man who would be free, who would be pure, who would live decently according to the laws of God and man.

The following seven principles by Leslie D. Weatherhead, M.A., author of *The Mastery of Sex,* bring healthy-mindedness within reach of all: (1) There is a way *through* the problem for all. (2) There is nothing unclean or disgusting about sex. (3) Accept yourself as a person having a sex instinct. (4) Realize that it is a God-given instinct, and that sex-desire is no more "wrong" than hunger at dinnertime. (5) At the same time, there *is* sex indecency about, and some have made it an occasion of filth (only in their debased minds). (6) In sexual adjustment there is a great place for the activities of the Christian Church. (7) We must confront men with Jesus Christ. "Whom the Son shall make free, they shall be free indeed."

Mere knowledge of sex cannot make possible the mastery of sex. It alone is possible through Him who said, "I am the way, the truth, and the life."

Some may comment, "Why drag religion into the sex question?" It is there already. Often there is no solution possible apart from religion. This supplies the dynamic force needed by the masses. All people need the cleansing stream of a renewed mind. Actually sex is a spiritual thing. It is hardly — unless circumstances bring disease — in the province of medicine and surgery. Purely scientific treatises do not go far enough, neither does psychology, that is, mere better mental behavior.

CHAPTER XX

CAPSULE INFORMATION

THE MICROSCOPE that enlarges several thousand times brings within sight of man a marvelous new world, and has proved that *life only comes from life.*

The latest experiments with mud, stagnant water, decayed meat, and so forth, have clearly demonstrated that no living cells develop from anything that is absolutely sterilized. In order for anything to be born, there must always be a living plant, a living animal, a living seed, or a living cell. Life comes from life. "In the beginning God created." This declaration, simple and sublime, still stands.

Scientists, in spite of their advanced knowledge of the process of human birth from the cell to the babe, do not know what life is. The Bible alone defines the source of all life, thus: *"In him was life."*

It is generally believed that the beginning of life is the joining of the egg cell from the female and the sperm cell of the male. Scientists figure out that the adult body has some twenty-six trillion, five hundred billion cells. These cells make up the various parts of the human body. What a *Master Mechanic* the Creator is!

The advancing knowledge of man concerning the wonders of the human body, its creation and its powers of reproduction, makes the inspired utterance of King David of Israel more comprehensible, *"I am fearfully and wonderfully made."*

Some, young people unfortunately suffer from *too much* sex information given *too early,* while others suffer from *too little* given *too late.* The middle-of-the-road way is best.

The organs of sex, wonderfully endowed with power: of reproduction, should not breed disgust in the youthful mind but should create a sublime awe because of their phenomenal abilities.

The two powers of the sexual organs are amazing. In the days of childhood and youth, they assist the body in the production of a suitable physical body; in the days of marriage they make possible the reproduction of human life; in old age the combined powers make for an attractive face and a magnetic personality.

The father and mother who give their sons and daughters a clean sex vocabulary, a pure conception of human birth, and a glorious outlook on marriage and home, have given them more than any millionaire can give his family as an inheritance.

The amazing wisdom and power of God, the Creator, are seen in that He made it impossible for any two human beings to be alike—not even quintuplets. Also, one of us is enough of us.

Would-be scientists who tried to tell us that man evolved from the ape have still to explain to us why the length of pregnancy of the monkey is 164 days, the baboon 169 days, and man 280 days. Slightly off schedule!

It is generally believed among students of the laws of inheritance that family traits are never lost by any individual absolutely even though there may be no family resemblance, or no similar personality traits. Nevertheless those qualities are carried down through all generations, hidden in the sperm and egg cells, and will reappear in children, grandchildren and future generations. It alone is the mercy of God that the evil traits have shorter life than the good. He has ordained that there shall be no fifth generation of these degenerates.

The "chromosomes" of the cells are supposed to be the agents which contain all the qualities of the ancestors. What a responsibility in living and in reproducing human life! Dr. F. D. Woods calls them "the most important things for their size in the world. They carry not only heredity, but determine color of skin, male or female, even color of hair."

The unborn child creates its own blood, according to the best authorities. Not one drop is transferred from the mother to the child. This with the inheritance settled at the moment of conception should allay the fear of pregnant mothers. Their only care needs to be concerned about themselves, their own health, and safety from undue physical force. Even that can never change the personality to be born. Many former fears were mere ignorant superstitions. It is difficult to injure a floating object. The unborn child floats in a large quantity of "water."

The best authorities state that the process of what determines the child's sex is settled at the first moment the sperm of the male and egg of the female meet. The process is simple, yet so little subject to human control that parents may never plan on having a boy or girl as they choose. Really, only the eye of the Eternal One sees what transpires, and He alone decides the type of personality and the sex.

Both man and woman have similar bodies, the same organs, eat the same foods, but the organs of sex exert such a far-reaching influence throughout the entire body that it is said: "Taken on the average, a man is a man to his thumbs and a woman is a woman to her little toes."

Walt Whitman writes: "The narrowest hinge in my hand puts to scorn all machinery, and the mouse is miracle enough to stagger sextillion of infidels." The vast array of facts about the complicated machinery of sexual parts and organs demand a Superb Craftsman. No wonder Jesus Christ, without explanation, majestically declared: "In the beginning God created them *male* and *female.*"

The modern dance was contrived to arouse the sexual nature and to give the passions reign without the reproof of reason or conscience. Locked together with one arm about a woman's waist, her breast against his, he places his foot between hers. To this must be added the sleeveless, low-necked dress exposing more or less of a woman's secondary sexual charms, her breasts. Evening, late hours, the intoxication of jazz music, warm air, clasped hands, and giddy whirl—charmed by these, the dancers cover from twelve to fifteen miles in an average evening's dance. These dancing centers are the feeder's of the brothel and lead to the downfall of many otherwise respectable girls.

Reaching boys and girls through the eye-gate and ear-gate, causing the downfall of millions, is such filth as, "Big Love Scene"; "A Beautiful Blond Woman in His Life"; "Could He Resist?"; "All of Me"; "Girls for Sale"; "Nudity in the Natural"; and hundreds of others equally vile.

Civilization, let alone Christianity, cannot survive so long as seventy million people, twenty-eight million being under twenty years of age, attend picture shows in the United States. The Editorial Council of the Religious Press surveyed the feature motion pictures released from January to the middle of May. The analysis revealed the fact of twenty-six plots built on illicit love; twenty-five plots on seduction; two on rape; one on incest; twenty-five characters were practicing, planning, or attempting adultery; three characters were presented as prostitutes; thirty-five major scenes were anti-moral. This is saying nothing about the murders, suicides, gangsters, and so on. *America, Whither Bound?*

"The shortest and surest route to the operating table for a young woman is to marry the young man who has lived a questionable life and saw no harm in sowing wild oats."—Rev. Oscar Lowry.

"Marriage with intentional childless homes through the practice of birth control is concubinage, not marriage."—Dr. Victor C. Pederson. To refuse to multiply is rebellion against the divine order in the moral universe.

The author of *A Virtuous Woman* presents the estimate of 2,000,000 illegal operations performed in the United States annually. Scores of thousands of women are being sent to their graves prematurely. These evil consequences make one shudder.

The universal damning double standard should have no place in the minds of thinking Christian people. What is wrong for a woman to do is wrong for the man to do. A man has no more right to drag himself through the quagmire of vice than a woman. A thousand times, No!

The brute side, the Edward Hyde side, of Dr. Jekyll is in every person. That is the reason for the apostolic injunction of Paul, "Make not provision for the flesh." Flirtation with sex evils downed Samson—the physical giant; Solomon—the intellectual genius; and David—the spiritual exemplar.

There is nothing low, funny, vulgar, degrading or vile even in the physical aspects of sex. Its proper study will not injure any pure man or woman, youth or child, for "unto the pure all things are pure."

What priceless memories cluster around the words "Father," "Mother," "Husband," "Wife," "Sweetheart" and "Child." Yet sex is the foundation of them all. These are the great words of our human life.

When some dame, damsel or sheik tempts to illicit affection and improper sexual relation, *Think! Think!! Think!!!* Two lives will be marred; a child may be born dead by reason of syphilis or with eyes blinded by gonorrhea.

Cautious physicians hesitate to speak dogmatically of curing syphilis in the sense that all germs in the system are killed. They speak of *arresting* the progress of the disease. Specialists generally recognize the standard for an ordinary case of treatment as being a minimum of two years or more of observation. *What a price to pay for a little sensual gratification!*

Roy E. Dickerson writes: "There is no permanent satisfaction, no true happiness, in sexual intimacies where there is *no* affection. It is a basic law of life."

Two beings suffer largely in illicit relations. The illegitimate child, which rarely knows a real home, suffers a cruel fate, and motherhood of the unwed is a dire disaster. It imposes a social stigma. This has led some to suicide.

If someday evil men will discover a one hundred per cent foolproof mode of birth control—illicit relations of the sexes apart from the risk of begetting children—these loveless indulgences will not make for happiness nor the best interests of society. That is the reason it is written, "Thou shalt not commit adultery."

The roadway to the deepest satisfactions in life is the one of self-denial and self-control which lead to self-realization. The roadway of so-called self-necessity is barred to happiness; it is wrong; it cheapens woman and degrades the man; it spreads vicious diseases; it summons children into the world under a social stigma and endangers the health of all concerned.

Writing in the *Survey*, Mary E. McChristie, referee

of Domestic Relations of the Hamilton County Court of Common Pleas of Cincinnati, says that in her interview with 600 cases who applied for divorce, 580, or 97 per cent, confided stories which indicated sex antagonism or sex maladjustment—a startling deduction and an eloquent cry for sane, wholesome sex education before marriage. Paul Popenoe expresses the same opinion in his book, *Conservation of the Family.*

PART VI

WHY THE STORY WAS TOLD

CHAPTER XXI

THE PATHWAY TO NOBLE MANHOOD AND BEAUTIFUL WOMANHOOD

> Consult the author's companion books to this
> one, *The Pathway to Noble Manhood* and *The
> Pathway to Beautiful Womanhood,* for a more
> complete discussion of the sex problems of men,
> women, young men and young ladies.

IN THIS CHAPTER we seek to point out the way to
Noble Manhood and Beautiful Womanhood. Both
parents and teachers of children and young people need
more than mere information to give to the rising generation. Altogether too often youth needs assistance
in rising to the standard of what they already know.
Social purity for many is the problem of *doing* what
they already know. Another category besides the uninformed is the defeated. Here are some suggestions:

Desire to be clean-minded. Thoughts can be directed
into high or low levels. We choose our ideals. None
will rise higher than they desire to rise. Purpose to
live clean; purpose to be decent.

Acquire a wholesome attitude towards sex. This attitude lays the foundation of a noble life. Pure thinking leads to clean living. Happy the child and youth

who heard the story of life for the first time from the lips of a good mother. Such begin life with a decided advantage.

Avoid unnecessary physical handicaps. Some physical factors make the battle for purity and decency all the harder. The sexual impulses are powerful. Proper eating, balanced meals, plenty of vegetables, greens, and fruit assist in controlled living. Leave alcoholic drinks alone; a drink or two will destroy your self-control. Tobacco in any form breaks down will power. Bathe frequently. Get sufficient sleep. Betimes, consult a physician of known good character.

Cultivate good social contacts. Do not be seclusive; be friendly. Make new friends and seek wholesome social contacts. Seek friendly association with men and women of high character who respect themselves. The commingling of the sexes of known good character makes for clean living. Sex tension is increased where there is the segregation of sexes. In association with the better class, lower sexual appeals and desires commonly are transformed.

Keep before you the desire of building a strong, beautiful physical body. Youth seeks to be the embodiment of a splendid physique. Sexual powers need not be a liability; they can be a tremendous asset. Physical energies can be dissipated or conserved. Stored-up energy can be released in other more noble directions.

The average girl desires to be beautiful. Sexual created energies properly controlled and focused make for a compelling magnetism. Female loveliness is strikingly displayed at puberty and afterward. The inner control makes its own imprint upon the face, yea, even upon the sprightliness of the step.

Sexual force has to do with all of life. It manifests itself in professional skill, in teaching ability, in powers of profound research, in wide-awake salesmanship, in art, in practical homemaking, in patience under test, in endurance, and otherwise. Self-control and mental accomplishments are interdependent to a large degree. The powers of thought are fed by the blood stream. During the days of strong sexual powers the memory is at its best and the mind keener.

The desire for a good name should be kept before youth. To be known as a clean-thinking, clean-mouthed, clean-living youth or maiden is no small attainment. This calls for manhood and womanhood. Sex-perverts are often disqualified for the best positions in life. Sexual degeneracy disqualifies also for a romantic courtship, which culminates in a desirable marriage and the setting up of a happy home.

The honor of parents is often at stake in the direction of social purity. Through the years many parents have sought to make the family name mean something worth while. By one act the name may be stained for years and years to come. Teach youth in the highest sense to salute their father and mother by a clean life and a good name.

Modesty is one of the outposts of chastity in the protection of the citadel of social purity. Immodesty is the want of modesty, delicacy, or proper reserve. Immodesty shows itself in inner thinking, conversation and deportment.

Keeping the mind occupied lays the foundation for a stable character. The occupied mind is usually the cleanest mind. Youth needs normal interests in educational directions. Youth also needs some avocations, better known as hobbies. These secondary interests, hobbies, take up some of the spare time. Hobbies vary. For some it will mean books, literary society work, birds, wild flowers, wood and metal working, and so on. The column could be well nigh as endless as human life interests.

Keeping physically active is a steppingstone to sex control. An occupation that calls for the expenditure of physical energies is the best outlet. The best outlet is hard work supplemented with active Christian work. Another outlet of secondary importance is recreational athletics. These should remain recreational rather than an enslaving sport.

Fragrant courtships must be planned. It often needs the counsel of interested parents. Intelligent courtship does not just happen; it is no mere coincidence. To many, courtship is only a time for "spooning," now called "petting." Certain matter-of-fact physical contacts are inevitable, and these cannot be considered as "petting" in the odious sense. For Christian young people there must be a line. This line should be drawn when physical contacts stimulate sexual desire unduly.

Young people of high ideals are challenged to plan for interesting evenings together, at home, away from home, and among friends. There is the reading of good books together, singing, music, candy-making, walks along pleasant lanes, drives, attendance at good pro- ·

grams, the normal church activities, indoor games which require skill, evenings spent with other young people, outdoor athletics, the normal community gatherings, and so on.

In your engagement days, learn to know each other better; become more intimate; discuss more intimate matters; plan for your future; complete your "hope chest"; and plan your finances.

Parents, teachers and others interested in the best of life must warn against the destructive places of amusement which fire the passions. Neither the theater, the movie, nor the modern dance, all created for pastime, cater to the clean, noble and fine things in life. They minister to the base passions. Any full-blooded young man or live young girl who frequents these places of amusement takes "fire in the bosom." The home is responsible in Christian circles to provide wholesome pastimes.

Those interested in directing youth in safe paths must bring to their attention the good effects of noble companions and the evil effects of bad associates. The associates will determine largely the character and the conduct. They may even determine the destiny.

The Bible counsels: "Iron sharpeneth iron; so a man sharpeneth the countenance of his friend." A young man who chooses companions whose ideals are low and whose morals are corrupted cannot escape the pollution that results from such associations.

Choose the young girl of ideals, whose lips are clean, whose life is pure, who does not condone the tainted story, tainted book, a tainted picture, a vulgar joke, or a low, foul insinuation.

Youth needs confidants, good counselors and intimate advisers. These confidants can be a mother, a father, a Christian doctor, or the pastor. Sex and related problems are perplexing. Then there is *God*—above all others—who knows youth better than they know themselves. The bent knee, the bowed head and the reverential heart will bring divine aid to any and all.

Home and a family are natural expectations. To keep these ideals of planning for a future home and family before youth is a steadying influence in the life. These ideals will also inspire. Young men should save some of their income for starting housekeeping; the young lady should fill her "hope chest." Fatherhood and motherhood are after all the goal of all true affections. It was so designed by the Creator. We train for other vocations in life, why not the greatest, *fatherhood* and *motherhood?*

The most needed and the deepest realization for young people is to be made of the fact that fatherhood and motherhood are the grandest and the noblest of all functions of sex. It is the highest purely physical act of which the human race is capable. This places human beings alongside the Creator of the universe. To bring into existence beings destined to endless existence. *What a responsibility! What a privilege!*

This calls for the product of pure love. Where restraint has been practiced, there will be a fuller satisfaction in marriage.

Young men and young women are assured on competent scientific authority that sex experience is not a necessity; it is not like muscles which need exercise. Continence is practical and healthful and is proved by medical men, physical trainers and members of exploring expeditions.

It is one of life's choicest satisfactions to take into your arms a boy or girl whom you know to have clean blood, the product of two pure lives, bone of your bone, flesh of your flesh; part of the one whom you have chosen as your own for life until death do you part. When this hour comes to your life, you will thank God, your parents for their pure lives, and all those who helped you on the high road of social purity.

It is unfair to expect a higher standard of self-control in women in matters of sex than in men. In the interest of their own health, honor and the future family, men must attain the same high standard they expect of women and girls. Sex appetite must either be indulged or controlled. If indulged outside the bounds of marriage, it is dangerous, dishonorable and damning.

The helps to a reasonable sex life for the young are: first, a physical regimen; hard work and active recreational interests make for bodily self-control; second, self-mastery is mental. The sex functions are under the control of the mind in man. This means the ruling out of amusements, interests, reading and conversation that turn the imagination to pictures of self-indulgence; third, the best and most powerful help is to cultivate a vigorous Christian life.

Some reader may say, "Such ideals are impossible."

That's true; no mortal man can live a life of absolute purity. "The ideal is beyond us. It's all well and good, but the standard is unattainable for us humans." Again, that's so. But God has made provisions to meet our deepest needs. In the "flesh dwelleth no good thing." God robed Himself in flesh and blood in the person of His Son Jesus Christ. In that body He died. He atoned for the guilt of our sins; His life met all the demands of holiness and purity. His death atoned for sin, and He now offers the gift of the Holy Spirit to all who come to God by Jesus Christ.

In closing, may we offer to you an open door to a clean, fresh, wholesome sex life. If you allow the Holy Spirit to fill, indwell, control your life, He will make these ideals possible — not only as ideals, but as a realization. Young man and youthful maiden, "Let Jesus come into your heart." Just now. May you and all the rest of us breathe this prayer from the lips of Charles Kingsley:

> *Exalt me with Thee, O Christ, to know the mystery of life, that I may use the earthly as the appointed expression and type of the heavenly, and by using to Thy glory the natural body, may be fit to be exalted to the use of the spiritual body. Amen and Amen.*

CPSIA information can be obtained at www.ICGtesting.com
Printed in the USA
BVOW01s1216050916

461162BV00001B/58/P